One Plus One

A Christian Perspective on Marriage and Family

STUDENT EDITION

Authors
**Stephen Endemano, David Bice,
Ollie E. Gibbs, Ed.D., and Sharon R. Berry, Ph.D.**

Design
Donna Harden and Robert Huff

One Plus One

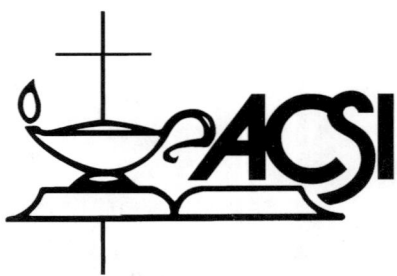

One Plus One: Student Edition
A Christian Perspective on Marriage and Family
Copyright, 1996

Association of Christian Schools International
P. O. Box 35097
Colorado Springs, CO 80935-3509
(800) 367-0798

Introduction

God Himself designed marriage and family as the foundations of society, as the training ground for each subsequent generation and as a source of enormous personal pleasure and satisfaction. With a current high divorce rate (in the general population), Christian marriages stand as testament to the happiness and success that can be achieved through commitment to Biblical principles. A study of these principles can prepare you to make good, informed decisions in the years ahead. As you purposefully choose God's side in the struggle against your own desires, some of your decisions will be tough. During these times, you can be assured that God's way is for your good and His glory.

An old adage says, "It takes a person of integrity to be a partner of integrity to be a parent of integrity." To this purpose the authors have developed this course. Their desire for you is in three areas.

• AS AN INDIVIDUAL — That you establish a deep personal relationship with the Lord, knowing His Word and being fully committed to obedience. From this foundation, that you become a person of assurance, clear direction, good relationships with others, a good sense of humor and a desire to serve.

• AS A PARTNER — That you wisely choose a life-long mate from the many friends you will have made. That you learn to share and nurture each other to become better as a couple than you could have been as singles.

• AS A PARENT — That you cherish the children God places in your care. That you provide for their needs physically, emotionally, educationally and spiritually, so that they, in turn, love the Lord and grow into responsible adults, able to accept leadership for their generation.

May God richly bless your time and effort as you study marriage and family from His perspective. May you grow individually, as you prepare to become a better person now and a better partner and parent in the future.

Table of Contents

Unit One

Unit Two

Unit Three

Unit One

Dating and Courtship

And the Lord God said, "It is not good that man should be alone: I will make him a helper comparable to him."

Genesis 2:18

Marriage should never just happen. It should be the most planned and well thought-out experience in your life. The progression of your dating relationships and the choice of your marriage partner will affect your future life, your attitudes, your interests, your friends, your career, and, most important, your relationship with God.

Marriage has been part of God's plan since He created Adam and Eve. It is so important in the Word of God, that, in the book of Revelation, John compares the marriage feast to a banquet in which believers partake as they enter eternity. Genesis through Revelation, God gives marriage and the family high

1

priority. In the same way, Christians realize that the decision of marriage is second only to the decision of personal salvation.

Many times, we often see marriage demeaned. Yet, it remains one of the most enduring institutions on earth. Look at the Sunday newspaper and count the number of people announcing engagements, being married and celebrating anniversaries.

One Plus One consists of three major parts: Dating and Courtship; Engagement and Marriage; and Marriage and the Family. We will look at the entire process from a Christian perspective.

Often couples in love believe that the marriage ceremony, with all of its formality and excitement, is the beginning and most important first step of marriage. Nothing could be farther from the truth. The marriage ceremony is one brief step in a long journey. The steps that precede and follow the "I do's" are the basis for a successful, lifelong Christian marriage.

One Plus One begins with the first step of awareness. This is a discomforting time of becoming acutely aware of the opposite gender. In recent times, it has become even more confusing, because young people receive mixed signals about their sexuality and about how males and females should approach relationships. Our first step is to look at the physiological and psychological differences between the sexes.

We will study misconceptions that have arisen about "what is right and wrong" because of liberal ideology and the non-Christian media. These misconceptions cause discomfort and confusion, but young people can overcome them by following God's standards.

The next topic will scrutinize dating and courtship. Essentially, dating is the period of eliminating, while courtship comes after prospective mates have made a commitment to each other. The former is one of exploration without long-term commitment. The latter is an in-depth period of learning about and revealing yourself to someone in whom you have a serious interest. The Christian must be aware of the possibility that any person he or she dates may become his or her spouse. During the dating and courtship steps, Christians should remember the "unequally yoked" admonition in 2 Corinthians 6:14.

Today, engagement has become a perfunctory, ring-on-the-finger process. However, it should be a time of realization for the Christian couple. This is the step during which couples make the commitment of spending their lives together and begin to establish the foundation for a solid marriage.

As the engagement proceeds, you and your fiancé must ask many questions. These include:

"Where will we live?"
"What financial resources do we have?"
"Will we both work?"
"How will we create a budget?"
"Which church will we attend?"
"Are we going to have Thanksgiving with
        your family or mine?"
"When will we want children?"
"How will we relate intimately?"

You can probe these and other questions during extensive talks, independent book studies, retreats and pre-marriage counseling with your pastor or a Christian marriage counselor. This must be an in-depth searching of yourself and your prospective mate before taking the life-commitment step into marriage. Engagement and marriage go together. You should not eliminate or ignore this critical process when establishing a life with the one you love.

Then comes the greatest step — marriage and family. This unification of two people is God's foundation for a family. A marriage is a time of sharing. You share successes, failures, good times, bad times, happiness, sadness, good health and illness. You also share the bathroom, the television, the clothes hamper, the money, the friends, relatives, and every conceivable event, emotion and experience. Most of all, you will share who you really are with someone else. When and if you have children, you will be sharing in even more expanding challenges and joys.

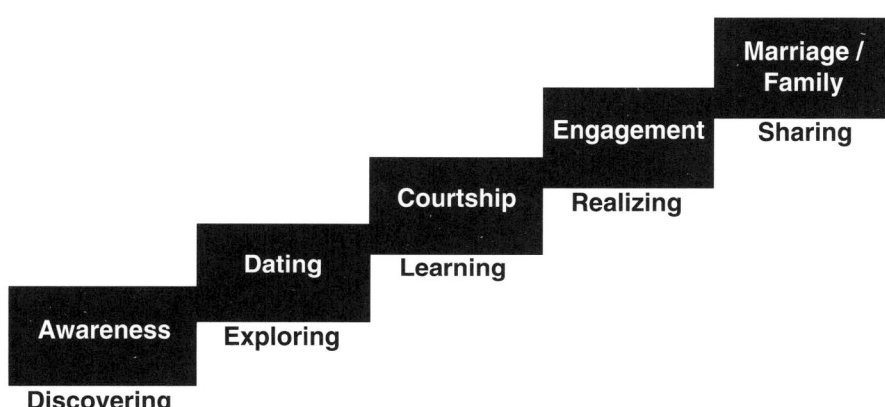

In summary, you will take these steps upward toward a fulfilling life as a married Christian. It is a great journey, and is worth your best efforts in preparation for this life-long commitment.

Understanding the Differences

So God created man in His own image, in the image of God He created him, male and female He created them.

Genesis 1:27

Introduction

A driving force in modern liberalism is the minimizing of the differences between the sexes. Many sociologists teach that differences between males and females have their roots, not in the biological/physical differences, but in early modeling, education and training of the two sexes. This fallacy has disrupted the courtship, marriage and child rearing of many couples and has crept into the thought processes of many Christians. It is important to know and respect the gender differences God designed in Creation. It is also important to be able to see through the false images of uni-sex sameness that the world wants to impose.

One Plus One

Fallacies of Sameness

The idea of sameness of the sexes is difficult to comprehend based on Scripture, especially Genesis 3:20. When Adam called Eve "the mother of all living," God had endowed her with several important bodily functions that no male will ever have — a rounder, purposely different body shape, a softer, more sensitive psyche and physique, monthly preparation for child bearing and the ability to bear and nurse infants. How can there be a sameness when fundamental physiological characteristics differentiate a woman from a man?

What are some of these differences? Actually, women and men differ in every cell of their bodies because of the X–Y chromosome differences. The two basic combinations of chromosomes create two entirely different sexes. These chromosomes are an intrinsic part of the male and female characteristics. No one can attribute their effects, realistically, to education and training.

Physiological Differences

You need only to take a cursory look to be able to see skeletal differences. Compare the fingers and hand structure of a woman. Her fingers are usually longer and more slender in relation to the palm and wrist. When you make the same type of observation of a man, you readily see that the opposite is true.

Most women have shorter legs, a longer trunk, a narrower waist, wider hips, a broader head with a less protruding chin and an overall tendency toward a shorter skeletal structure.

A man's thyroid gland is smaller and less active than a woman's, and her thyroid enlarges slightly when she is menstruating or pregnant. Because of the differences in size and activity, this gland has some significant effects on women. Women are more prone to have goiters, but more resistant to cold. A woman's thyroid causes smooth skin, a relatively hairless body and plays a role in the changes of emotions she experiences. She will laugh, cry and hug over situations in which most men remain stoic.

Men, on the other hand, have more brute strength, endurance and larger lungs. Males have 20 percent more red blood cells than females. Their average heart beat rate is 72 per minute, versus 80 for women, but their blood pressure is ten points higher on average than females.

Men and women have different types of endurance. On a daily basis, most men can work longer, lift more and run faster. Yet, over their lifetimes, women have stronger constitutions. Women have fewer heart attacks, fewer high blood pressure problems and a longer life expectancy than men. Virtually every insurance age chart in the United States shows that women outlive men by a three to four year average.

Bible Truths

God originated marriage and the family to accomplish His purpose and to meet man's needs.

Genesis 1:26, 28; 2:15 - God's purpose.

26 Then God said, "Let Us make man in Our image, according to Our likeness; let them have dominion over the fish . . . fowl . . . cattle . . . all the earth, and over every creeping thing that creeps upon the earth." 28 And God . . . said to them, "Be fruitful, and multiply, and fill the earth, and subdue it: and have dominion . . . " 15 Then the Lord God took the man and put him in the garden of Eden to tend and keep it.

Genesis 2:18, 20-25 - Man;s need

18 And the LORD God said, "It is not good that man should be alone; I will make him a helper comparable to him . . . 20 But for Adam there was not found a helper comparable to him. 21 And the LORD God caused a deep sleep to fall on Adam . . . 22 Then the rib which the LORD God had taken from man He made into a woman, and he brought her to the man. 23 And Adam said: "This is now bone of my bones and flesh of my flesh . . . "

24 Therefore a man shall leave his father and mother and be joined to his wife, and they shall become one flesh.

Psalm 68:6

God sets the solitary in families . . . .

Proverbs 18:22; 19:14

22 He who finds a wife finds a good thing, and obtains favor from the LORD. 14 . . . a prudent wife is from the LORD.

1 Corinthians 11:8-9

8 For a man is not from woman, but woman from man. 9 Nor was man created for the woman, but woman for the man.

Encyclopedia of Bible Truths for
School Subjects
Dr. Ruth C. Haycock © ACSI

Psychological Differences

Physiological differences are often the more obvious differences between men and women. However, they are not nearly as complicated, and perhaps not as important in stable courtships and marriages as the psychological and emotional characteristics. In his book, *What Wives Wish Their Husbands Knew about Women*, Dr. James Dobson explores the psychological needs of women and the ways men can meet these needs. These needs do not change as a relationship matures from courtship through a lifelong marriage. They are an essential component in all three stages. Couples must not ignore them as they take the initial steps and then the journey through this lifelong commitment.

For example, while romance may just be a pleasant way to provide a fond memory for a man, it is a necessity for a woman. Spouses must identify early, and continue to consider,their psychological differences. These differences create complementary partners. Two persons fit together in God's plan for successful marriages.

Men find much of their self-esteem in the achievements they attain — career success, a new car, sports ability and other measurable things. Romance and love are an essential part of a woman's self-esteem. A man will remember his first car and its horsepower. A woman remembers when she first received flowers and from whom she received them. Who do you think remembers the football schedule and forgets the marriage anniversary? It is not the person who fondly recalls what each wore at the time of the marriage proposal. Females need the tender thoughts shown by cards, flowers and candy. Males respond more to being honored and exalted.

Abigail VanBuren, in her newspaper advice column, *Dear Abby*, once asked how important sex versus romance was to her female readers. In an amazing response by over 100,000 women, 72 percent said they found more satisfaction in being held than in having intercourse. In a subsequent request for male responses, 67,000 men replied. Only 5,600 believed that being held was more important than sex. This is a major contrast. The hold, the touch, the loving words and the small gifts are the lifeblood for a woman in dating and marriage.

Wives and husbands have different psychological needs concerning the home. Men need the home as a retreat from the competitive world they face each day. They look for a tranquil base, devoid of conflict. An old chair in a certain spot is fine with most men. Women look at the home and everything in it with a more loving view. Matching furniture, new drapes, rearranging things and "making a house a home" are important to women. The home is part of a woman's psyche, while it is a refuge for a man. This difference in the view of the home has led to problems and conflicts as more women have entered the competitive workplace. While the psychological needs have remained the same, the economic needs or wants have changed, forcing many women to struggle with the priorities of home and career.

Summary

As you date, become engaged, marry, and create your family, it is important to realize that even as you become one, differences remain. You must learn to respect and enjoy the different needs of your partner. God intends for you to be happy when you marry. He expects you to respect and care for the spouse He has chosen for you. Celebrate the wonderful differences that males and females have in God's perfect plan.

Challenge Your Thinking

I. **Bible Link**

A. Locate four verses in the Bible that prove God made men and women to be different.

1._____   2._____

3._____   4._____

B. What two commands did God give to both Adam and Eve in Genesis 1:28?

_____

_____

C. Many people place these commands in the categories of creating products and nurturing people. How did God design men and women to fulfill these commands?

_____

_____

_____

D. What important function did God give to Eve in Genesis 3:20?

_____

_____

Understanding the Differences

II. **Comprehending the Lesson**

   A. List five physiological differences between males
      and females.

   Males   Females

   _____   _____

   _____   _____

   _____   _____

   _____   _____

   _____   _____

   B. List five psychological differences between males
      and females.

   Males   Females

   _____   _____

   _____   _____

   _____   _____

   _____   _____

   _____   _____

III. Writing

A. Write one paragraph explaining why you believe God created men and women to be so different.

_____

_____

_____

_____

_____

_____

_____

_____

_____

_____

_____

_____

_____

B. Write one paragraph explaining why it is
    important to understand the psychological
    differences between the sexes as you begin your
    steps toward marriage.

_____

_____

_____

_____

_____

_____

_____

_____

_____

_____

_____

_____

2

Maintaining God's Principles

*And do not be conformed to this world, but
be transformed by the renewing of your mind, that
you may prove what is that good and acceptable
and perfect will of God.*

Romans 12:2

Introduction

Each day young people face a world that
believes virtue and virginity are no longer
important. Many people have abandoned
God's principles of lifetime commitment in
marriage. They now scorn these principles
and use them as humor in the media. The
liberal media pushes to see how far it can go in
language, dress and illicit sex by putting worldly values in attractive packages. Even Christians come to
accept the innuendoes and sensuality that slowly
erode God's standards.

Abandoning Virtue

An oxymoron the media, especially television, has presented to the American public is the phrase, "wholesome family entertainment." This implies that the programs available in the early evening are wholesome and suitable for all family members. Although this may have been true in the 1960's, it is far from true today. It is difficult to find a television program that does not offend the principles of God.

A study conducted between 7:00 P.M. and 9:00 P.M. on a Wednesday illustrates the immoral program themes. Four situation comedies on major television networks had five cases of intercourse without marriage, two homosexuals, seven incidents of divorce, two examples of extramarital affairs and one case of sexual misconduct by a supervisor with an employee. The theme of one program was the correct etiquette for a man following a "one night stand" when he did not want to see the woman again. The resolution was to buy her a good breakfast. The writers did not appropriately address the implications of out-of-marriage sexual activities.

Sexual Revolution

The 1960's brought a great sexual revolution. In less than 25 years, many people abandoned a 4,000 year-old moral code instituted by God. That is not to say that immorality had not existed in the world, but for the first time in modern history, promiscuity became openly accepted and even revered.

Maintaining God's Principles

Media personalities, teachers and even religious leaders have endorsed sexual relationships of every kind. Nothing is taboo, because, "It inhibits personal growth and self-esteem." Some mainline churches perform marriages of homosexual couples, and support the right of adoption by these couples. Liberals have redefined the word "family." It is now any group of people that merely thinks of itself as a family, rather than a group bound by the special bond of blood or matrimony.

Some leaders consider divorce, out-of-wedlock pregnancies and homosexuality as examples of healthy diversity and pluralism. In their 1995 annual meeting, representatives of the largest teacher's union in the United States, the National Education Association voted to declare October as National Gay, Lesbian and Bi-Sexual Month for public schools.

American society is paying the penalty for turning its back on God's Word. Sexually transmitted diseases abound. The Center for Disease Control report that 25 percent of sexually active teenagers will contact a venereal disease before completing high school. Genital herpes, an incurable disease, affects over 20 million Americans. The AIDS epidemic kills thousands of Americans each year and threatens the entire world. Millions of girls, even eleven- and twelve-year-old children, are having babies out of wedlock. Many people view abortions as an acceptable form of birth control. Abortions done on teenage girls account for most of all the pre-born children who are killed each year. The bumper sticker is true that states, "The Most Dangerous Place in America Is in a Mother's Womb."

Justifying Wrongdoing

We have allowed the media and the world to use euphemisms to justify wrong actions. Illicit sexual intercourse is "safe sex," "going to bed" and "fooling around." Homosexuals are "gays" and not condemned for engaging in an unnatural act. Non-Biblical companionship gains respectability under the phrases: "Alternative lifestyles," "Significant other," and "A relationship."

Magazines, movies, television, recordings and radio publicize the decline of moral values in a positive light. They now give space to people and practices which were considered immoral by the American public as recently as 25 years ago. One magazine has devoted eight pages to "the pleasure and pressures of sex at an early age," but has not once condemned the practice of premarital sex by teenagers. One 15-year-old, unmarried Houston girl with a ten-month-old son says she, ". . . used to be real bad, but motherhood has improved her life." A seventeen-year-old boy boasted that his life in New York has improved since he has accepted being a homosexual and is no longer lonely.

In Massachusetts, the Superior Court gave a 13-year-old girl permission to have her second abortion. Planned Parenthood had provided an attorney for the girl whose case was decided in minutes. The stories continued with a twelve-year-old from California having had her first sexual encounter right after watching Saturday morning cartoons. One girl in Florida did not want to give in to her boyfriend and kept her virginity during eight months of dating, but finally agreed to have sex for fear of losing him. None of the boys involved expressed any remorse or found anything wrong with their actions.

The magazine had photographs of the couples smiling. All the accounts portrayed the actions of these preteens and teenagers as normal. Only the 17-year-old girl from Florida expressed any regret. She knew that when her boyfriend goes to college he will forget her and find other girls. Not one sentence in the entire eight pages related to the concept of right or wrong. The writer did not devote a paragraph to the psychological or physical results of the immoral actions of these young people. There are always many serious consequences from immoral acts — hurt feelings, guilt, incurable diseases such as AIDS and genital herpes, unwanted pregnancies, and most important, God's condemnation. The one obvious message in the article was that safe sex does not exist outside of marriage.

Bible Truths

Sexual activity outside of marriage is condemned by God and brings with it serious problems within the home.

Exodus 20:14; Deuteronomy 5:18

The seventh commandment:
14 You shall not commit adultery.

Leviticus 18:20; 20:10-12

20 Moreover you shall not lie carnally with your neighbor's wife, to defile yourself with her.

2 Samuel 11, and 12:1-23

God condemned David's sin with Bathsheba, through he was the king. David repented and God still used him.

1 Corinthians 5:1-11

Paul instructed the church at Corinth to discipline a man guilty of fornication.

1 Corinthians 6:13-20

13 . . . Now the body is not for sexual immorality but for the Lord, and the Lord for the body. 16 Or do you not know that he who is joined to a harlot is one body with her? For "The two," He says, "shall become one flesh." 18 Flee sexual immorality . . . 19 Or do you not know that your body is the temple of the Holy Spirit Who is in you, Whom you have from God, and you are not your own? 20 . . . Therefore glorify God in your body.

Galatians 5:19-21; Ephesians 5:3, 5; Colossians 3:5; 1 Thessalonians 4:3, 4; Hebrews 13:4, and many other passages.

Encyclopedia of Bible Truths for
School Subjects
Dr. Ruth C. Haycock © ACSI

Peer Pressure

According to the secular media, the deterioration of morals has occurred in almost all young people. Newspaper articles, polls of teenager opinions and studies done by the Center for Disease Control in Atlanta report high incidences of illicit sexual activity. In one report from the CDC, the Center stated that 54 percent of high school students have had sexual intercourse. The 1990 study reported a 40 percent rate of sexual activity in ninth graders. At the tenth grade level, it was 48 percent. By the eleventh grade, it was 57 percent, and by grade twelve, the study reported 72 percent of teenagers having had sex.

A Time/CNN poll reports a major reason for teenagers to engage in illicit, premarital sex is to be more popular and/or impress friends. Fifty-eight percent of the teenagers polled cited this peer pressure as the reason for early sex, while another 49 percent said they succumbed to pressure from dates.

Christian Home, School and Church Influence

These types of reports paint a discouraging, devastating portrait of future of families in America. However, there is substantial evidence that these statistics do not present a true picture of all teenagers. In a 1990 survey conducted for the Association of Christian Schools International (ACSI), the Barna

One Plus One

Research Group shows that Christian school students' attitudes about sex and morals are substantially different than those of public school students. This confirms what many Christian school educators have long believed. Students enrolled in Christian schools have a solid moral base not reflected in studies based on students in public and secular schools. As one 16-year-old female in the survey said, "It's hard because it seems like all teenagers are categorized together. If you are a teenager . . . people assume things of you. Some won't even look at your testimony."

The survey asked students about the acceptability of reading pornographic literature, watching "X" rated movies, engaging in premarital sex, homosexuality, heavy petting on dates and other immoral activities. When asked if it is sometimes all right to read pornographic literature, 95 percent of Christian high school students said it is not. The same percentage said it is unacceptable to watch "X" rated movies. Ninety-nine percent of these students replied that homosexuality is never right.

In a repudiation of the world view that a majority of American teenagers are sexually active in high school, 87 percent of the Christian school students said they had never had sexual intercourse. The same percentage replied that sex before marriage is wrong, even if the two people believe they love each other. Nine out of ten of these students believed heavy petting to be wrong, and 99.7 percent said that abortion is wrong. An anomaly in these statistics is that, while nine out of ten said they had never had sex, more than six out of ten said other students were having sex. It appears that people have misconceptions about the sexual activity of their peers.

The survey reveals the important influence of family, church and Christian education on the students. A full 93 percent described themselves as having been saved; 94 percent attend church at least once a month. Seven out of ten are in a church youth group, attended Sunday school and have personal devotions. Most of these students came from two-parent homes with 70 percent saying that their household members attend almost every church service. If these students have attended Christian schools for more than three years, almost three-quarters of their friends attend Christian schools, which probably reduces worldly peer pressure.

The influence of home, school and church is illustrated in the statistic that 90 percent of Christian school students share — the belief that God absolutely forbids homosexuality, premarital sex and abortion. Eight out of ten students who received their information about sex from their parents, their church or their Christian school were strongly opposed to premarital sex. Many Christian school students appreciate this influence. One 17-year-old Christian school coed stated, "We have more problems than you realize. We know what is right and wrong, but some areas of our lives are never addressed. We appreciate input from our churches and schools."

Solid Belief in God's Standards

Christian school students do not waver in their belief in God's standards. They believe that many actions are either expressly forbidden in Scripture or that they are wrong according to Biblical principles. Nine out of ten of these students say that God forbids homosexuality, premarital sex, abortion and stealing.

According to 70 to 77 percent of the students in the survey, cheating, drug use, suicide and pornography are forbidden by God. Twenty-five percent say that these actions are wrong in principle. Almost 40 percent consider heavy petting to be forbidden by God; another 50 percent believe it to be wrong in principle.

Christian school students are less influenced by television than the general teenage population. A. C. Nielsen, a television viewing statistics company, reports that the average teenager watches more than 22 hours of television per week. The ACSI survey revealed that two-thirds of Christian school students claim to watch fewer than ten hours of television per week. Another 22 percent of these students say they watch a maximum of 15 hours. Only four percent responded that they equal the 22-hour national average.

Summary

It is necessary to be able to objectively look at the way in which the world has attempted to suborn God's Word. Television programs that hide sin in humor tend to decay the moral standards of young people. Magazines that celebrate sport personalities living together out-of-wedlock emphasize the popularity of the people involved and not the sin. Teachers, who define homosexuality as an alternative lifestyle, ignore the Biblical condemnation of this unnatural way of life.

Organizations which promote abortions as a method of birth control deny the sanctity of life. Movies that encourage premarital sex ignore the teachings of the Bible. God has set the standard and wants what is best for His children. When you obey His Word you are able to resist the changing morals of the world and the pressures of the media.

Challenge Your Thinking

I. **Bible Link**

A. How does Romans 12:2 relate to to the way in which the media influences opinions and actions?

_____

_____

_____

B. Use the following references to describe what God has to say about sexual sin.

1. Genesis 13:13; 18:20; 19:4-24; Romans 9:29; and Luke 17:29.

_____

_____

_____

_____

2. Exodus 20:14; 1 Corinthians 9:27; 10:8

_____

_____

_____

_____

3. Proverbs 7

_____

_____

_____

_____

4. 2 Peter 2:18

_____

_____

_____

_____

5. Romans 3:31

_____

_____

_____

_____

One Plus One

II. Comprehending the Lesson

A. Check the box beside those things which have resulted from the sexual revolution and the abandoning of God's moral code.

❑ AIDS
❑ neglected children
❑ more broken homes
❑ legalized abortion
❑ better TV programs
❑ less promiscuity
❑ more premarital sex

❑ abused, battered women
❑ increase in pornography
❑ lower rate of sexual diseases
❑ more unwed mothers
❑ acceptance of homosexuality
❑ fewer divorces
❑ use of euphemisms such as, "alternative lifestyle"

B. What two sexually transmitted diseases are incurable?
1._____ 2._____

III. Writing

A. Explain how the use of euphemisms gives false respectability to immoral actions.

_____

_____

_____

B. Select one of the young people described in the magazine about "the pleasures and pressures of sex at an early age" and write that person a letter of advice from a Christian perspective. Use a separate sheet of paper.

Choosing the
Right Mate

*Can two walk together, unless they are
agreed?*

Amos 3:3

Introduction

Speaker and author Josh McDowell has said,
"Everyone a person dates is, however remotely, a
candidate for marriage." His words are important to
remember when you ask for, or accept, a date.
There is certainly no question, in our society,
that the step of dating is the most common
method for young people to explore and
develop relationships with members of the
opposite sex. Dating is one of the steps in
selecting a marriage partner. Christians and non-
Christians date, but the standards, goals and activities should be distinctively different for Christians.
The question you need to keep asking yourself is:
"Would the Lord be pleased with my dating
relationship?"

One Plus One

Dating Patterns

Patterns you establish during your dating period continue, and may intensify, should you marry. It is unrealistic to believe you will be able to solve persistent problems in a dating relationship after marriage. A person who has bad habits during the dating process, does not automatically reform after saying, "I do." Researchers have clearly shown that problems and irritants before marriage do not disappear; instead, they frequently intensify.

It is through dating that you begin to explore relationships with the opposite sex. You begin to understand how males and females interact with each other. This is the beginning of intimacy. For the Christian, it is important to move through this bonding and selecting process slowly and with strict limitations. There is no need to hurry a dating relationship. Also, there is no need to allow the "starry eyes" of emotional infatuation to overwhelm your good judgment in building a committed relationship.

Qualities and Attitudes

Because your date may become your mate, it is essential that you have some idea of the type of person you would like to marry. Everyone has different ideas about what are the best qualities in a person. Physical qualities may appear to be the most important in dating, but personal qualities are what more often determine happiness with that person.

It is a good idea to list the qualities that are important to you, not what your friends think. Your dates must always be Christians. They must be thoughtful, virtuous, responsible, truthful, affectionate, honest and forgiving. "You shall know them by their fruits," is God's standard as presented in Matthew 7:16.

As you compile your list of important traits, remember that you must look closely at the people you date to see if they actually exhibit the traits you consider valuable. During the dating period, people tend to have a facade that may conceal bad habits. There must be outward manifestations of the qualities you have chosen for those you date, not just a wish list of how you hope they will be after you reform them. Following are some of the traits that could be on your list.

A person with a positive attitude is happy and content. When a positive person plays a game and loses, he does not pout or get angry at the winner. It does not take "things" to give this person joy. This person does not try to find fault in others or be unfairly critical.

One who is thoughtful will place the needs of others before his or her own and finds happiness in serving others. Thoughtful people respect the emotional and physical needs of others. They remember events that are important to you without being constantly reminded.

Contrary to the belief of many in our society, virtue is not old-fashioned. The virtuous person is pure in body and in mind. What type of language does your date use at school, at a ball game, with friends when you are not around, or when he with you? Does your date try to pressure you to do things with which you are uncomfortable? Does your date suggest that you watch "R" rated movies? Mind pollution can lead to disrespect of the opposite sex.

Is your date always late? Do you have to help your girlfriend with her homework at the last minute? Does your boyfriend misplace things all the time? Does your date drive carelessly and ignore traffic laws? Is your date constantly using the excuse, "I forgot"? These signs of irresponsibility can cause problems as a relationship develops.

Truthfulness engenders trust, which is one of the absolute building blocks of a good marriage. Untruthfulness in a person you are dating is a danger sign that you must not ignore. Remember, someone who exaggerates or covers an untruth by giving only partial information, in reality, is being untruthful. Manipulative behavior has its roots in untruthfulness, as a date tries to control you or make you do or say something with which you are uncomfortable.

The ability to express love through words and action is vital to an intimate relationship. You should look for tender words and actions that are natural and appropriate throughout the day, not just in private to initiate petting. A difficult task in the dating process is to distinguish between true affection and that affection shown you as a tool to entice sexual favors. An affectionate person shows tenderness and warmth to those family members and friends to whom they are close.

Honesty is part of being truthful. However, in today's society many people believe there are degrees of honesty. When a store clerk gives you and your date too much change back for a purchase, what do you do? What do you say when your date boasts about copying cassettes from a friend? Would you accept lying and stealing as a fundamental part of your marriage?

An integral part of all relationships is forgiveness. As a Christian, one must follow Jesus in His teachings of forgiveness. Does the person you are dating say he or she forgives you, only to reintroduce your transgression later? If so, he or she lacks a forgiving attitude. Do you have to keep saying "I'm sorry!" to the person you are dating? A forgiving relationship does not include burdening one's companion with guilt.

Bible Truths

The choice of a suitable marriage partner is a matter for prayer and concern, whether for oneself, or for one's children.

Exodus 34:15-16

God warned Moses against covenants, marriage or other relationships with heathen nations. *15 Lest you make a covenant . . . and they play the harlot with their gods and make sacrifice to their gods . . . 16 And you take of his daughters for your sons, and his daughters play the harlot with their gods . . . .*

Deuteronomy 7:2-6

God commands Israel not to marry the heathen, nor to allow their children to do so, lest they turn from God.

Ezra 9:12

Ezra reviews God's command which Israel had broken again and again: *12 Now therefore, do not give your daughters to their sons; . . . and never seek their peace or prosperity, that you may be strong and eat the good of the land, and leave it as an inheritance to your children forever.*

2 Corinthians 6:14-18

14 Do not be unequally yoked together with unbelievers. For what fellowship has righteousness with lawlessness.

Genesis 24

Abraham's great care in the choice of a bride for Isaac.

Genesis 38

Judah married a Canaanite. Their firstborn, Er, was so wicked that God slew him (v. 7).

1 Kings 11:1-8

1 But king Solomon loved many foreign women . . . 2 . . .from the nations of whom the LORD had said to the children of Israel, "You shall not intermarry with them, nor they with you. For surely they will turn away your hearts after their gods." Solomon clung to these in love. Verses 4-8 tell the results.

Encyclopedia of Bible Truths for School Subjects
Dr. Ruth C. Haycock   © ACSI

A solid relationship cannot be built only on intense and fleeting emotions. You and your date are likely to spend a great deal of time together. Therefore, the sharing of interests is essential. What recreational activities does he or she enjoy? Given an hour of free time, would you prefer to jog, work a jigsaw puzzle, listen to music or play a board game? If one of you prefers solitude over the other's company or begrudgingly gives in to the other's interests, it is probable that you are not right for each other.

Christianity

The most important quality you must look for in those you date is their personal relationship with Jesus Christ. Salvation involves a commitment to God, which radically changes a person from inside out. A Christian will be more likely to follow the Spirit-filled life of love, joy, peace, patience, gentleness, goodness, faith, meekness and temperance of Galatians 5:22–23 than a non-Christian. You must beware of the people who act spiritual just to win your affection. Many people say they love the Lord, while their actions fail to demonstrate their love.

Summary

There is no such thing as casual dating. Each dating experience adds to your understanding of the complex relationship between the sexes. As you take dating steps, remember that each date is a potential lifetime spouse.

One Plus One

Challenge Your Thinking

I. Bible Link

A. What messages are conveyed about choosing a mate in the following verses?

1. Matthew 7:16, 20

_____

_____

2. Galatians 5:22-23

_____

_____

3. 2 Corinthians 6:14-15

_____

_____

4. 1 Corinthians 5:9-11

_____

_____

B. How does the word "walk" in Amos 3:3 apply to dating and marriage?

_____

_____

_____

Choosing the Right Mate

II. Comprehending the Lesson

A. List ten qualities you would want the people you date, and possibly mate, to have.

1. _____   2. _____

3. _____   4. _____

5. _____   6. _____

7. _____   8. _____

9. _____   10. _____

B. List ten traits (or characteristics) you would not want the people you date, and possibly mate, to have.

1. _____   2. _____

3. _____   4. _____

5. _____   6. _____

7. _____   8. _____

9. _____   10. _____

III. Writing

A. Select four of the positive qualities from those you listed and explain why they are important to you.

1. _____

_____

_____

_____

2. _____

_____

_____

_____

3. _____

_____

_____

_____

4. _____

_____

_____

_____

B. Write one paragraph either agreeing or disagreeing with the statement by Josh McDowell, "Everyone a person dates is, however remotely, a candidate for marriage."

_____

_____

_____

_____

_____

_____

_____

_____

_____

_____

_____

How to Be a Great Mate

But the fruit of the Spirit is love, joy, peace, long-suffering, kindness, goodness, faithfulness, gentleness, self-control. Against such there is no law.

Galatians 5:22-23

Introduction

Sometimes you may believe you are unwanted and unloved, but God considers you a person of immeasurable worth. Genesis 1:26 teaches that God made you in His image. John 1:12 and Romans 8:14 say that if you are a Christian you are a child of God. The precious blood of God's Son, Jesus Christ, purchased your salvation. Jesus would not have died for you if you were not important to Him. When you think no one cares for you, remember, God does care.

This same principle applies to others. God created them in His image; you must respect that. You should neither disrespect nor defile the other person as you take steps leading to marriage.

Inward Character

We live in a society that tries to make us believe that external things are all important. Society measures a person's worth through beauty, strength, clothes, achievement and material possessions. It is wrong to believe that if you have these things, you are important. God does not base worth on outward appearance, but on inward character. This concept must be part of your judgment of others as you date and prepare yourself for being a great mate. Just as you do not want people to evaluate you only on your external characteristics, you should not judge members of the opposite sex based upon worldly values.

You are now developing qualities that will make you a great mate in the future. You must be secure and comfortable within yourself and have a good Biblical self-image. This is important because your expectation of someone else to improve your self-esteem will create an unhealthy emotional dependency.

> # WORK ON "ME" FIRST!
>
> ## A Great Me + A Great Mate = A Great Marriage

Interdependence

Marriage counselors, Dr. Les Parrott III and Dr. Leslie Parrott, point out from Proverbs 27:17, "As iron sharpens iron, so a man sharpens the countenance of his friend." Marriage will hone and improve you, but neither it nor your spouse will make you whole. Marriage brings oneness to two people, not sameness. You must be yourself, or you will end up dependent upon your partner for continual support. You will live in an "enmeshed" relationship. This relationship will lead to ". . . low self-esteem and a sense of inferiority that is easily controlled by . . . one partner."

Drs. Parrott continued by stating that a "disengaged" relationship, the opposite of an enmeshed one, is also bad. Here, the spouses isolate themselves and strive toward total independence. This is an attempt to compensate for feelings of inferiority. You cannot be married and live a life separate from your spouse.

The proper relationship is one of interdependence, in which the partners treat each other with self-respect and dignity. Each person nurtures his or her own individual spiritual growth as well as that of the partner. People who make great marriage partners do not have to be married to be happy. They are happy being themselves. They are complete in Jesus Christ and are comfortable with themselves. In his book, *Loneliness: the Fear of Love*, Ira J. Tanner says, "Any attempt to mold our

Bible Truths

Relationship to God and obedience to Him must have priority over family relationships.

Genesis 12:1-3
    God called Abram to leave his family and homeland to go to a new location unknown to him.

Genesis 22:1-14
    For many years God had promised Abraham a son through whom should come One Who was to bless all the earth. When God called on Abraham to offer him as a sacrifice, Abraham obeyed and God intervened in his behalf.

Deuteronomy 13:6-11
    Under the Law, God commanded: *6 If your brother, the son of your mother, your son or your daughter, the wife of your bosom, or your friend . . . secretly entices you, saying, Let us go and serve other gods . . . . 8 You shall not consent . . . .*

Matthew 10:34-37
    37 He who loves father or mother more than Me is not worthy of Me. And he who loves son or daughter more than Me is not worthy of Me.

Matthew 12:46-50; Mark 3:31-35; Luke 8:19-21
    When Jesus' mother and brothers wished to speak to the Lord, He said: *48 . . . to the one who told Him, "Who is My mother and who are My brothers?" 49 . . . He stretched out His hand toward His disciples and said, "Here are My mother and My brothers! 50 For whoever does the will of My Father in heaven is My brother and sister and mother.*

Luke 14:26
    The love of a disciple for the Lord is meant to be so great that, in comparison, love for family members seems like hate.

Encyclopedia of Bible Truths for School Subjects
    Dr. Ruth C. Haycock © ACSI

Enmeshed   **Interdependent**   **Disengaged**

mates in an effort to match them to our fantasies is arrogance on our part and an insult to them."

Mature Decision Making

When you have a close relationship with God and a good self-image through His salvation, you are able to face life realistically. You should not allow anxieties and neurotic behaviors that avoid dealing with problems. Most neuroses begin with a feeling of inadequacy. Ordinary daily problems threaten everyone. If the response is to avoid these, the defense mechanisms used to avoid the problems become significant conflicts themselves. These types of reactions can intensify when you establish a relationship with someone of the opposite sex.

A person who consistently makes bad decisions certainly develops a negative self-image. It is important to begin developing the skill of making mature decisions. Mature decisions result when individuals deny immediate self-gratification and carefully consider all the options and possible results. A mature decision maker does not form a conclusion until he has all the information needed and has weighed the consequences of various options.

Part of mature decision making is to realize that two people can make opposite choices. This is because we base decisions on values and needs. People who are dating, or in any stage of a relationship, have different "values" and "needs" that may conflict. You can lessen "value" type decisions by both of your being Christian and basing your values on the Bible. "Need" type decisions between two people require acceptance of the other person's right to have different needs. Remember that males and females have differing psychological and emotional needs.

You can begin to evaluate your decision making ability by asking yourself some questions and answering them honestly:

"Am I clear on goals for my life?"
"Am I willing to deny myself immediate
        gratification to insure long term goals?"
"Have I established friendships with people
        who are a positive influence on me?"

Positive answers to these questions suggest that you can make mature decisions.

Personal Relationship with God

As you take the steps toward marriage and becoming a mate, it is important to have a personal relationship with the Lord. A good relationship with God does not guarantee a good marriage relationship, but it will help immensely. When couples can pray together, share promises from Scripture and seek direction based on Biblical principles, they have a major advantage over those who do not.

Christian people create Christian homes. There is a clear pattern — Christian individuals become Christian partners. You cannot, however, consistently date non-Christians and suddenly find yourself in a Christian marriage. Neither can you learn to deal with problems in a Christian manner if the people you date are not Christian. There are problems in married life. You are better equipped to cope with these problems if you have explored problem solving in the dating and courtship steps.

Summary

In order to become a great mate, you must first examine yourself. When you are able to make mature decisions and understand the value of yourself and your prospective mate, you will be able to sustain a marriage. When you then wrap a good marriage in Christianity, you will be able to overcome the obstacles and temptations the world places in the way of marriage.

Marriage is neither a dominance of one partner over the other, nor a union based on the independence of each partner. It is a union with husbands and wives as heirs together of God's grace — equal in importance and potential as evidenced in 1 Peter 3:7.

One Plus One

Challenge Your Thinking

I. **Bible Link**

    A. How does each of the following verses show your importance to God?

        1.   Genesis 1:21 _____

               _____

        2.   John 1:12 _____

               _____

        3.   Romans 8:14 _____

               _____

    B. List each of the Fruit of the Spirit from Galatians 5:22-23. Then in one sentence for each give an example how you are fulfilling the fruit.

        1. _____

           _____

           _____

        2. _____

           _____

           _____

3. _____

_____

_____

4. _____

_____

_____

5. _____

_____

_____

6. _____

_____

_____

7. _____

_____

_____

8. _____

_____

_____

9. _____

_____

_____

II. Comprehending the Lesson

A. List the four qualities given to help you achieve being a great mate.

1. _____ 2. _____

3. _____ 4. _____

B. Compare and contrast an enmeshed relationship with an interdependent one.

_____

_____

_____

_____

_____

_____

_____

III. Looking at Myself

A. Read the following statements that are based on four qualities of a great mate. Use the 1-10 rating scale under each statement to rate yourself by circling the number that reflects your beliefs. One is "seriously doubt" and 10 is "strongly believe."

I am confident that God loves me and has a special plan for my life.

1   2   3   4   5   6   7   8   9   10

I believe I can live in a relationship based on self-respect and dignity.

1   2   3   4   5   6   7   8   9   10

I have the ability to make mature decisions.

1   2   3   4   5   6   7   8   9   10

I have a commitment to develop a close personal relationship with God.

1   2   3   4   5   6   7   8   9   10

B. Research indicates that people with a good self-image respond better to their spouses. In answering the following questions, check the box most appropriate to your feeling.

One Plus One

1. Do you consider and respond to the needs of others?

   Always ⟵——————————⟶ Never
   ❑   ❑   ❑   ❑   ❑

2. Do you think of yourself as equal to others?

   Always ⟵——————————⟶ Never
   ❑   ❑   ❑   ❑   ❑

3. Are you confident that you can deal with problems?

   Always ⟵——————————⟶ Never
   ❑   ❑   ❑   ❑   ❑

4. Do you have values and principles which you will defend without compromise?

   Always ⟵——————————⟶ Never
   ❑   ❑   ❑   ❑   ❑

5. Do you have a wide range of emotions and desires that you accept as part of yourself?

   Always ⟵——————————⟶ Never
   ❑   ❑   ❑   ❑   ❑

6. Do you resist worrying about the future?

   Always ⟵——————————⟶ Never
   ❑   ❑   ❑   ❑   ❑

7. Do you accept the fact that you make errors and mistakes?

   Always ⟵——————————⟶ Never
   ❑   ❑   ❑   ❑   ❑

8. Do you act on your decisions and judgments even if others disagree or ridicule?

Always ⟵—————————————⟶ Never

❏　　　❏　　　❏　　　❏　　　❏

9. Are you able to accept compliments without exhibiting false modesty?

Always ⟵—————————————⟶ Never

❏　　　❏　　　❏　　　❏　　　❏

10. Do you speak about your religious beliefs in the presence of non-believers?

Always ⟵—————————————⟶ Never

❏　　　❏　　　❏　　　❏　　　❏

Premarital Counseling

Without counsel, plans go awry, But in the multitude of counselors they are established.

Proverbs 15:22

Introduction

William L. Coleman begins his book, *Before the Ring*, with, "If you were planning a two-week trip through the Rocky Mountains, you would be asking hundreds of questions. What's the best way to get there? What will the weather be like? What clothes should I take? How much will it cost? Where will I stay? How many places will I have time to visit along the way?"

It is a sad fact that most couples prepare better for a vacation than they do for the lifetime journey of marriage. Two people may be "in love" but not necessarily prepared for marriage. Proverbs 12:15 says, "The way of a fool is right in his own eyes, but he that heeds counsel is wise." That is not to say that people in love are fools, However, good sense dictates that they seek counsel before taking the next step on their journey.

One Plus One

Phases of Contact

Marriage counselors are often amazed that otherwise well-informed people are ignorant about marriage. How can this be? One explanation is that we cannot agree on a proper time or place to teach young people about marriage. Is it at home? School? Church? Is twelve or 20 the correct age? Another explanation for the ignorance is that a myth exists that it does not require any special knowledge to live together as a married couple. It is a serious misconception to believe that marriage and living together, "comes naturally." We see that this is not true simply by the number of failed marriages in America today. Christians must see their obligations to do everything possible to ensure long-lasting, happy marriages.

Your growing relationship can extend to the courtship and engagement steps. Each of you is seriously learning about the other. You must realize the implications of your commitments. These two steps are a dangerous period, which must be approached with care. Do not be embarrassed to seek advice about your feelings and emotions. Christians, in this age of indiscriminate and premarital sex, must realistically discuss the phases of intimacy. Christians have invaluable resources in their pastors and Christian counselors. You should also read books by Christian authors and discuss them with your prospective mate.

Dr. James Dobson, in *Love for a Lifetime*, notes that the phases of contact proceed through twelve progressive periods. The first nine set the stage for marriage intimacy, while the last three are postmarital. A couple passes through the first seven phases during the period of awareness and dating. These stages are named for the type of visual and physical contact engaged in by couples. These are eye to body, eye to eye, voice to voice, hand to hand, hand to shoulder, hand to waist and face to face.

The seventh phase, "face to face," involves close personal space, as couples talk, laugh and maintain eye contact. It also includes hugging and kissing. It is the final phase of the dating and courtship steps. A couple at this point, who have not skipped any of the previous phases, will be able to communicate with few words. Each will begin to know the other's thoughts. Here begins sexual desire, which is a normal step in the progression of the relationship. Unfortunately, this is a time when many couples compromise their moral values because they believe they have a commitment to each other.

Couples should go through the phases sequentially to lay the foundation for commitment. When a couple skips a stage, it can lead to premature contact and eliminates the fun of learning about each other progressively and thoroughly. It is similar to flying across the country rather than taking a train. The

Love or Infatuation

Infatuation leaps into bloom. Love usually takes root slowly and grows with time.

Infatuation is accompanied by a sense of uncertainty. You are stimulated and thrilled, but not really happy. You are miserable when he is absent. Love begins with a feeling of security. You are warm with a sense of nearness, even when he is away. Miles do not separate you.

Infatuation says, "We must get married right away. I can't risk losing him. Love says, "Don't rush into anything." You are sure of one another. You can plan your future with confidence.

Infatuation has an element of sexual excitement. If you are honest you will discover it is difficult to enjoy one another unless you know it will end in intimacy. Love is the maturation of friendship. You must be friends before you can be lovers.

Infatuation lacks confidence. When he's away, you wonder if he's with another girl. Love means trust. You may fall into infatuation, but you can never fall into love. Infatuation might lead you to do things you'll be sorry for, but love never will.

Love leads you up. It makes you look up. It makes you think up. It makes you a better person than you were before.

—Unknown Author

plane passenger reaches his destination quickly. The passenger on a train experiences the joy and beauty of the trip.

Phase eight, "hand to head," is an extension of phase seven, but with emotional closeness as familiarity grows. This phase does not involve intimate touching but provides for "comfortable closeness." Now a couple enters the engagement step. After these two steps, a couple probably enters phase nine of "hand to body" which becomes much more intimate. No couple should pass farther than phases eight and nine before marriage.

Couples usually go through the romantic, exploratory learning time of their relationship much easier than the factual, realizing step, but both steps can be disastrous if the couple handles them improperly. A wise couple seeks counseling and advice from a pastor or a pre-marriage counselor. It is the time to look at what makes a happy marriage and how you and your future spouse will achieve that goal.

Myths of Marriage

Almost all marriage counseling books and seminars discuss marriage myths. These false ideas about how life will be after marriage are the cause of many of the problems that later occur. The overriding myth of marriage is the belief in a happily-ever-

Bible Truths

Marriage is not essential to live a godly and useful life; God has a place for single people.

Jeremiah 16:1-4

There are times when God directs to a life without a spouse and children. God spoke to Jeremiah: *2 You shall not take a wife, nor shall you have sons and daughters in this place.*

1 Corinthians 7:7, 32-35

In the light of the coming persecution and then the coming of the Lord, Paul urges the unmarried to remain unmarried, even as he is; yet he recognizes that this is not God's will for all. *7 . . . But each one has his own gift from God, one in this manner and another in that. 32 . . . He who is unmarried cares for the things that belong to the Lord— how he may please the Lord. 33 But he who is married cares about the things of the world — how he may please his wife. 34 There is a difference between a wife and a virgin. The unmarried woman cares about the things of the Lord, that she may be holy both in body and in spirit. But she who is married cares about the things of the world — how she may please her husband. 35 And this I say to your own profit . . . that you may serve the Lord without distraction.*

1 Corinthians 9:5-6

Paul points out that both he and Barnabas were unmarried, but other apostles were married. God has a place for both.

Revelation 9:5-6

During the Tribulation period, God has a special work to be done by 144,000 Jews chosen by Him. All will be chaste, unmarried men.

Encyclopedia of Bible Truths for School Subjects
Dr. Ruth C. Haycock © ACSI

after life. Everything will not necessarily be all right. Remember, you have not been constantly happy with your relatives, your friends or your coworkers. Your potential spouse has also not been pleased with relatives, friends and coworkers all the time. Why should your being in love assure your mutual happiness? You must realize that marriage requires every moment of every day of your life. You and your mate see one another from a different perspective than before marriage, when you appeared more vibrant and happy.

Counseling can help you realize that the intense, passionate, romantic love that you have at the time of the wedding will diminish, and it will be replaced with a deeper, abiding intimacy. When we observe the one we love, we see an idealized image. A comedian once said that her husband never belched during their dating, engagement or honeymoon. When he finally did, it almost knocked her down. She did not stop loving him, she just realized he was not perfect. He was a human being.

With counseling, you can achieve a realistic view of the lifelong commitment you are making. You should enter counseling during the courtship step and complete at least one-half of it before publicly announcing your engagement and marriage plans. This will allow you the opportunity to withdraw if there are irreconcilable differences.

One Plus One

One problem area that couples tend to pretend does not exist is money. Larry Burkett, a Christian financial advisor, says, "Money is either the best area of communication in a marriage or its worst." The idea that money does not matter in a marriage is a myth. Money does matter. You can have too little, too much or just the right amount. Yet, it can still be the source of problems in marriage. Counseling can help you to see how the Bible approaches financial responsibilities.

Summary

Marriage is a wonderful relationship designed by God. Frank Minirth of the Minirth-Meyer Clinic states, "Couples will have much more fulfilling marriages when they begin to realize how many factors influence a happy marriage." You and your prospective mate must not only be in love; you must look at marriage realistically. You must plan for your life, not just hope that your marriage will be one that lasts.

It is not a sign of weakness of character or faith to want to prepare for marriage. Counseling by Christian advisors will help you and your prospective mate plan for a lifelong commitment. Do not hurry through courtship and engagement. Enjoy this time of learning about each other, while realizing the importance and responsibility of marriage.

Challenge Your Thinking

I. Bible Link

A. How do Proverbs 12:15 and 13:10 relate to William L. Coleman's introduction in his book *Before the Ring*? "If you were planning a two-week trip through the Rocky Mountains, you would be asking hundreds of questions. What's the best way to get there? What will the weather be like? What clothes should I take? How much will it cost? Where will I stay? How many places will I have time to visit along the way?"

_____

_____

_____

_____

B. Read the Book of Ruth. Observe the courtship and marriage of Boaz and Ruth. How does God's plan in this marriage relate to Jesus and your salvation?

_____

_____

_____

II. Comprehending the Lesson

A. Place the premarital phases of contact in order within the proper steps to marriage.

1. Awareness/Dating

   _____

   _____

   _____

2. Courtship/Engagement

   _____

   _____

   _____

B. List three places a Christian couple can seek pre-marital counseling.

1. _____

2. _____

3. _____

III. Writing

A. Explain why the courtship and engagement are dangerous periods of time for Christian couples.

_____

_____

_____

_____

_____

B. List two marriage myths and explain why they must be overcome for a happy marriage.

1. _____

_____

_____

2. _____

_____

_____

Unit Two

Engagement and Marriage

For this reason a man shall leave his father and mother and be joined to his wife, and the two shall become one flesh.

Ephesians 5:31

Marriage is the most significant relationship God has given to mankind. God ordained the wondrous union of Adam and Eve in the Garden of Eden. ". . . a man shall leave his father and mother and be joined to his wife. . ." (Genesis 2:24; Matthew 19:5; Mark 10:7-8; and Ephesians 5:31). These passages denote a separation from parental dependence and the forming of a strong bond of unity, permanence and intimacy with a spouse. The marriage union is a reflection of Christ's relationship with us after we receive Him as personal Savior.

One Plus One

R. C. Sproul notes that in Genesis 2:24-25 and I Corinthians 7:1-7, God defines the characteristics of a good marriage. These five characteristics are:

- Each person must be willing to leave his or her mother and father to establish an independent unit.
- Each person must commit to a lifelong relationship.
- A man and woman must obey civil law and become legally married in the eyes of the state.
- A couple must become one flesh, through a sexual relationship.
- A couple must follow God's pattern for roles and responsibilities.

A Christian marriage is a total commitment of two people to Jesus Christ and to each other. Marriage is often the refining process God uses to conform us to the image of Christ and develop us into the person He wants us to be.

"Being in love" alone is insufficient to sustain a happy marriage. Though intense at first, a couples' passion mellows over the years and their relationship changes. Couples must objectively look at what will happen in their lives after the marriage ceremony. Successful business people like to repeat the warning, "If you fail to plan, you plan to fail." God has instituted marriage for you; now you must take the responsibility of planning to make it work and survive.

6

What Is Marriage?

So then they are no longer two but one flesh. Therefore, what God has joined together, let not man separate.

Matthew 19:6

Introduction

You can look up the definition of marriage and find, "The state of being husband and wife." The definition does not say much about romance, nor does it really tell you about marriage.

Daniel Freeman gives insight into the meaning of marriage in *Why Get Married?* He says, "Is marriage a private action of two persons in love, or a public act of two pledging a contract? Neither, it is something other. Very much other! Basically, the Christian view of marriage is not that it is primarily or essentially a binding legal and social contract. The Christian understands marriage as a covenant made under God and in the presence of fellow members of the Christian family. Such a pledge endures, not because of the force of law nor the fear of its sanctions, but because an unconditional covenant has been made. A covenant more solemn, more binding, more permanent than any legal contract."

You, as a couple, will establish this covenant with God and you must do everything you can to protect it. There will be problems, but you must learn to solve them.

Defining Marriage

A 19th century writer described marriage as being similar to a pair of scissors. Thee parts are joined so that they resist separation. They move in opposite directions and punish whatever comes between them. In this analogy, the writer described a permanent marriage, which allows differing opinions and always resists those who would break up the relationship.

Authors Wes Roberts and H. Norman Wright say, "A Christian marriage is a total commitment of two people to the person of Jesus Christ and to each other. It is a commitment in which there is no holding back of anything. Marriage is a pledge of mutual fidelity; it is a partnership of mutual subordination. At the same time, it can be a refining process that God uses to mold us into the man or woman He wants us to become."

Marriage can be described by scrutinizing the cycles. A man and woman unite to begin a shared life. They create a home and start a family. Each of the two has his or her own tasks, but cooperates to make the household work. They rear their children. Then the children leave to marry and begin the cycle again. Thus, the institution of marriage is the foundation of the family and society.

Three Types of Love

Every good marriage has love, but what is this thing that poets write about? When you and your fiancé marry, you will begin to realize three different types of love: eros, philia and agape. Each has its place in your lives and will help define your marriage.

Eros is the name of the Greek god of love and has come into our language as the love that seeks sensual expression. It is the romantic and sexual love defined through our biological beings. Though eros is not a Biblical term, according to Proverbs 5, Song of Solomon and Hebrews 13:4, a good marriage includes this type of love.

Friendship love is part of philia. A husband and wife must be friends and companions. Philia is the love that allows us to communicate and cooperate. When you see a married couple walking hand in

Bible Truths

The marriage relationship is designed to picture the union of Christ and the church, and husband and wife as one in God's eyes.

Ephesians 5:22–33

Several aspects of the union of Christ and the church are pictured: the submission of the church to Christ its head, the sacrificial love of Christ for the church, the desire of Christ to perfect and sanctify the church and the union between Christ and the church.

Genesis 3:22–24

When God looked for man in the garden, and later when he expelled Adam and Eve from the garden, He spoke of the man, but obviously meant both of them. *22 Then the LORD God said, "Behold, the man has become like one of Us . . . 23 therefore the LORD God sent him out of the garden . . . 24 So He drove out the man . . .* In 4:1, they were obviously together.

1 Corinthians 11:11–12

11 Nevertheless, neither is man independent of woman, nor woman independent of man, in the Lord. 12 For as the woman was from the man, even so the man is through the woman; but all things are from God.

Ephesians 5:28

So husbands ought to love their own wives as their own bodies; he who loves his wife loves himself.

Encyclopedia of Bible Truths for School Subjects
Dr. Ruth C. Haycock   © ACSI

hand while engaging in conversation, they are experiencing philia.

Christ's love is the highest form of love. This sacrificial and gift love is unconditional and eternal. Agape, the self-giving love, is Christ's model for us to follow in marriage. You must make agape happen. It is an action verb. You must do something: an act of kindness, a thoughtful word or a forgiving spirit. When you practice agape, the needs of your spouse will become more important than your own.

Agape and philia are necessary for a long-lasting marriage. They are what make eros exciting and fulfilling. A marriage based on eros alone has little prospect of survival. Physical attraction is a minor part of a real love life and will not sustain a marriage over a lifetime.

Fulfilling Needs

Abraham Maslow, a psychologist, created a pyramid structure of levels of need. Maslow listed these needs in five categories: physical needs, security, love and belonging, esteem and self-actualization. He diagramed these in order of importance. Basic needs are at the base of the pyramid, while the highest level of psychological need is at the top.

Physical needs represent those things necessary to sustain life. You need oxygen, water and food in order to live. Safety and security are those things you need to keep you from harm. These can be many things, including a warm house, clothing and door locks. Beyond physical safety, there is the need for psychological security. This includes significant people you can trust, and predictability and order in your environment. The third level of love and belonging defines the need for affection and affirmation from others. The next level is esteem needs. Here, a person develops an internal sense of being worthwhile and having a place and purpose in the

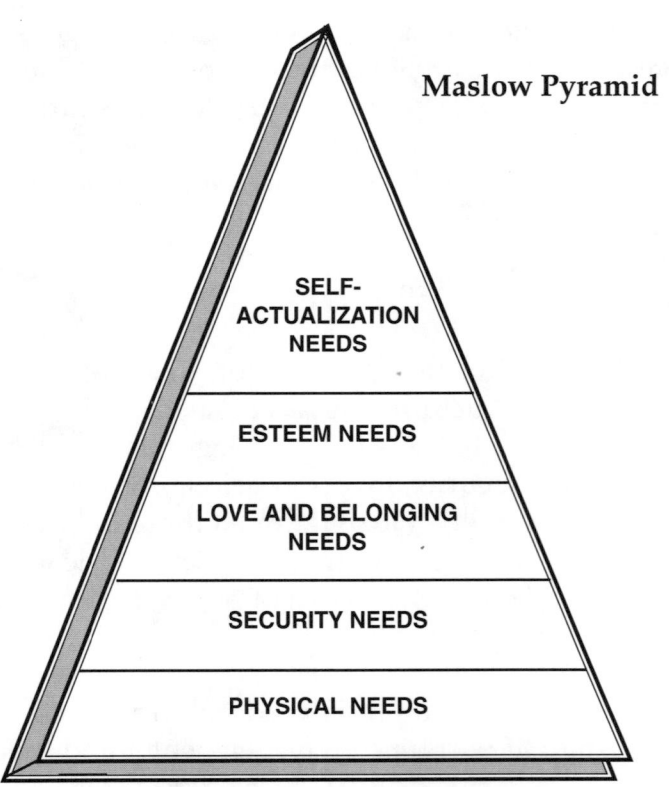

Maslow Pyramid

SELF-
ACTUALIZATION
NEEDS

ESTEEM NEEDS

LOVE AND BELONGING
NEEDS

SECURITY NEEDS

PHYSICAL NEEDS

world. As all these needs are met, a person becomes a mature, creative individual, capable of fulfilling his own God-given potential.

In addition to the basic needs of life, marriage also fits into the total pyramid. The problem is that many marriages fulfill only the needs of the first two levels. Being a "good provider" is an example of meeting these minimal needs in a marriage. A husband and wife will provide each other with money, food, housing, transportation, and other basic needs pertaining to security. It is in the top three needs of love and belonging, esteem and self-actualization that many mates fail. The Maslow Pyramid on the previous page illustrates the ways in which a husband and wife can help each other develop to full potential.

Summary

Marriage is fulfilling your spouse's needs under the loving guidance of Jesus Christ. You cannot help your mate to become complete, if you are not whole yourself. Wholeness comes only through salvation and Christian growth. Christian marriage satisfies all basic needs and all three types of love through an unconditional covenant between the couple and Jesus Christ.

One Plus One

Challenge Your Thinking

I. Bible Link

A. Write a paragraph based on Genesis 2, 1 Corinthians 7 and Ephesians 5 describing what God has to say about marriage.

_____

_____

_____

_____

_____

_____

_____

_____

_____

B. Ruth (Ruth 1:16-17) gives perhaps the most beautiful statement of commitment in all literature. Her statement is not about marriage, although many couples use it in the wedding ceremony. Do you believe it is appropriate? Why or why not?

_____

_____

_____

_____

_____

_____

_____

_____

One Plus One

II. **Comprehending the Lesson**

A. Give the definition of each of the three types of love. Then name a person who exhibits or has exhibited that particular love.

<u>Love</u>	<u>Definition</u>	<u>Person</u>
eros	_____	_____
	_____	_____
philia	_____	_____
	_____	_____
agape	_____	_____
	_____	_____

B. Complete the Maslow Pyramid on the following page with the five categories of needs. Then write in two examples for each that you believe should exist in a marriage.

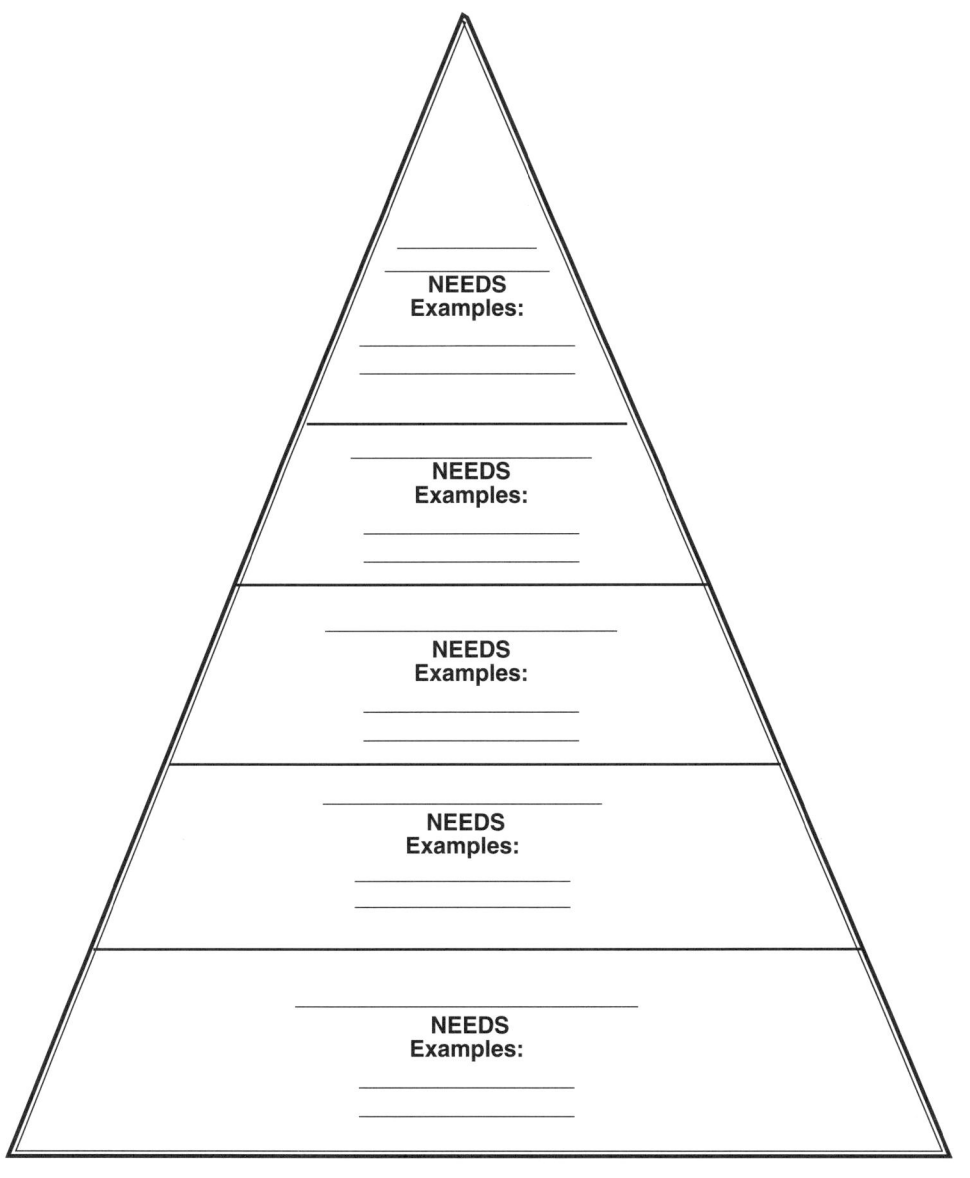

NEEDS
Examples:

NEEDS
Examples:

NEEDS
Examples:

NEEDS
Examples:

NEEDS
Examples:

One Plus One

III. Writing

A. Why are strong marriages important to the structure of society?

_____

_____

_____

B. In this chapter, there are two descriptions and an analogy of what marriage is. In your own words, write a paragraph giving either an analogy or a description of marriage.

_____

_____

_____

_____

_____

_____

Maturity

7

When I was a child, I spoke as a child, I understood as a child, I thought as a child; but when I became a man, I put away childish things.

1 Corinthians 13:11

Introduction

Every child dreams about becoming an adult. Young people see growing up as being able to do anything they want to do, whenever they want to do it. Although they do not realize it, they sometimes fail to understand the responsibilities that will come with adulthood. Adolescents frequently are in conflict with their parents over issues such as being treated as adults. Adolescents have not necessarily achieved maturity simply because they look, think and act as some adults do.

Transition from Childhood to Adulthood

The transition from childhood through adolescence to adulthood is not an easy journey. A poor family situation, poor role models, poor advice or a poor understanding of how to make this transition can make the journey even more difficult. Many people are unable to make the transition. Although they grow up physically, they remain mentally and emotionally immature. Maturity is an integral part of a successful marriage.

Achieving Independence

The teenage years are difficult for both you and your parents because of the split between dependence and independence. This means that the focus and amount of control is shifting. It is not usually a smooth transition and often changes several times a day. The continuous adjustment may keep everyone a little "off balance" in communicating and relating to each other.

Even after the teenage years, parents and children will continue to make adjustments in their relationships with each other. What began as total dependence when you were a baby will slowly change, as you mature, to the point at which you are self-supporting but still seeking advice from your parents.

Because of the difference in perspective, teens and parents often have difficulty in communicating. The following illustration provides some understanding of the problem.

Maturity

Incident 1	Teen comes home from school	
Parent says	"How was your day?"	
Teen Frame of Mind	**Independence**	
Gist of Teen Perception and Response	"You're being nosy. Why do you want to know everything? Don't you trust me? I can take care of myself."	
Gist of Parent Perception and Response	"I was just making conversation but I will refrain from asking in the future."	

Incident 2	Teen comes home from school another day	
Parent Action	Smiles but remains silent	
Teen Frame of Mind		**Dependence**
Gist of Teen Perception and Response		"You don't care what happens to me. Don't you know I've had the worst day of my life? You are insensitive and cold-hearted."
Gist of Parent Perception and Response		"I'm confused. The other day you said I was being too nosy, but today you say I don't care about what happens to you."

Different Toys

It is often said that one difference between men and boys is in the cost of their toys. This humorous view of the maturity exhibited by some, contains much truth. When Paul says, "I put away childish things," it is to this concept that he is referring. Maturity lies not in one's ability to purchase more expensive toys. It lies rather in the knowledge that there are more important things in life.

The same is true of marriage. Many children "play house" when they are little. Children usually base this play-acting around imaginary meals and dressing up as adults. It is far from the reality of marriage. However, some couples retain that immature view. They fail to turn away from and discard their childish thinking.

Marks of Maturity

A mature person can be easily identified. He or she will exhibit the following characteristics.

1. One's basic beliefs and values are established. He or she understands what is important and why, and is committed to living in harmony with these values. For a Christian, this means committing his or her life to Christ, being conformed to His character and obeying His commands.

2. One accepts personal responsibility for actions, is self-controlled and self-motivated to behave in accordance with values and goals. He or she is self-disciplined in handling frustrations and disappointments. In this area, the Christian lives under the direction and conviction of the Holy Spirit.

3. One maintains an accurate view of self and personal abilities, handles problems well, is emotionally stable and keeps a positive attitude toward life. According to Philippians 4:4-9, Christians believing in the care and sovereignty of God have both the Peace of God and the God of Peace abiding within them.

4. One delays gratification, commits to long-term goals and projects, understands that rewards of correct decisions and actions often come after several years and accepts the knowledge that the best rewards are often intangible. These include good health, happiness, peace of mind, pleasure in a job well done and gratification in helping others. The ultimate reward for a Christian is Heaven.

5. One's interests focus on the good of others rather than self, does those things that benefit spouse and children, improve society and serve humanity. The mature Christian is especially motivated to love others and to represent Christ in the world.

6. One establishes open, warm relationships with others, is responsive to the needs of others but is not overly dependent on their approval, can solve interpersonal conflicts without anger or violence, has a good sense of humor and follows through on commitments. Christians endeavor to love God first and then to love their neighbors as themselves.

There is a major distinction between being a mature adult and being a legal adult. You have only to pass a certain number of birthdays to legally achieve adulthood. Mature adulthood, however, requires thoughtful planning and preparation.

Maturity in Marriage

Even the most mature adults experience times of challenge and struggle in their marriages. This is because of the complexity of the marriage relationship. A husband or wife must be willing to place the needs of the other first. Only mature adults behave in this manner, which is the reason maturity is a necessity in a successful marriage.

In his book *Understanding Ourselves as Adults*, Paul Maves gives eight characteristics that indicate mature adulthood. It is important to note that he begins each of these characteristics by placing responsibility on the individual.

The individual —

- has completed a basic education.
- is able to physically separate from parents.
- has become financially self-supporting.
- accepts responsibility for personal actions.
- is capable of making wise decisions.
- views himself as an adult, and others agree.
- seeks adult friendships.
- knows how to maturely deal with conflict.

All of these characteristics are important in mature adults. However, many marriage counselors believe that one's willingness to accept personal responsibility is probably the most significant factor. Children blame others; mature adults accept responsibility for their own actions.

Accepting Responsibility

Every choice or decision has consequences. Immature people try to escape those consequences. Irresponsibility for personal actions and choices began in the Garden of Eden. Adam blamed Eve because she gave him the forbidden fruit. Then he blamed God for having given him Eve. Eve placed the blame on the serpent. Neither Adam nor Eve accepted the fact that each of them had chosen to disobey God's command. God did not accept their

Bible Truths

Parents and children must have a mutual respect for one another.

Children must give their parents a place of honor and respect, and parents must be sensitive to the needs and feelings of their children.

Exodus 20:12; Deuteronomy 5:16; Matthew 15:4; 19:19; Mark 7:10

12 Honor your father and your mother, that your days may be long upon the land which the LORD your God is giving you. 16 . . . and that it may go well with you.

Leviticus 19:3, 32

In verse 3, the Lord relates respect for parents to the fact that He is holy. *32 You shall rise before the gray headed and honor the presence of an old man, and fear your God.* The emphasis here is on respect for age and maturity.

1 Kings 2:19

Solomon's example even as the king. When his mother entered to request a favor, he rose to met her, bowed to her and set her a place of honor.

Psalm 103:13-14

God likens His concern for us to that of a father, one who understands his children's limitations. *13 As a father pities his children, so the LORD pities those who fear Him. 14 For He knows our frame; He remembers that we are dust.*

Proverbs 19:26: 23:22; 28:24; 30:17

God uses some plain language in emphasizing the many kinds of respect that should be shown to parents. *26 He who* mistreats his father and chases away his mother is a son who causes shame and brings reproach. 22 Listen to your father who begot you, and do not despise your mother when she is old. 24 Whoever robs his father or his mother, and says, "It is no transgression," the same is companion to a destroyer. 17 The eye that mocks his father, and scorns obedience to his mother, the ravens of the valley will pick it out, and the young eagles will eat it.

Jeremiah 35:18-19

God promised special blessing to the Rechabites because they obeyed their father's command.

Malachi 1:6

God uses the typical son's honoring his father to illustrate the incongruity of Israel's disobedience in failing to honor Him, the heavenly Father.

Matthew 18:6, 10

Offending a child, or despising a little one, is considered by God a serious sin. Better that a person be drowned than to sin in this matter.

Ephesians 6:1-3

1 Children, obey your parents in the Lord, for this is right. 2 "Honor your father and mother," which is the first commandment with promise. 3 "That it may be well with you and you may live long on the earth."

Colossians 3:20

Children, obey your parents in all things, for this is well pleasing to the Lord.

Ephesians 6:4; Colossians 3:21

4 And you, fathers, do not provoke your children to wrath . . . . 21 Fathers, do not provoke your children, lest they become discouraged. Here is warning against the danger of expecting the impossible from children, of constantly nagging until they feel they can never please, of teasing or sarcasm which takes advantage of their limitations.

Encyclopedia of Bible Truths for School Subjects
Dr. Ruth C. Haycock   © ACSI

excuses. Instead, He told them the consequences of their actions.

In the book, *Secret Choices*, the authors Dr. Ed Wheat and Gloria Okes Perkins write, "Because our first ancestors rebelled at God's gracious design for their lives, that same rebellion has now spilled over into our own minds." This makes it easy for us to avoid making decisions and to blame others for our poor decisions. It is part of our Adamic nature. How do we achieve the maturity to avoid following this pattern? God has given us the freedom to make choices, the most important of which is to accept salvation though Jesus Christ. Once we have made that choice, He will help us in all of our decision making.

Summary

Philippians 4:13 says, "I can do all things through Christ, who strengthens me." When you accept this in your marriage, you can approach all decisions with a mature outlook. God has given the Bible to you as a manual that will lead to making good choices based on His Word. The closer one comes to full maturity, the greater capacity he or she has to experience all of God's blessings. Paul says in Philippians 3:13-14, "Brethren, I do not count myself to have apprehended; but this one thing I do, forgetting those things which are behind and reaching forward to those things which are ahead, I press toward the goal for the prize of the upward call of God in Christ Jesus."

Challenge Your Thinking

I. Bible Link

A. Match each of the following Bible verses with the appropriate characteristic of maturity. Write out the verses and the characteristics they match.

1. 1 Kings 3:28 _____

_____

_____

    Characteristic _____

_____

2. Proverbs 27:23 _____

_____

_____

    Characteristic _____

_____

3. Acts 7:22 _____

_____

_____

Characteristic _____

_____

4. Ephesians 5:31 _____

_____

_____

Characteristic _____

_____

5. Philippians 2:20 _____

_____

_____

Characteristic _____

_____

6. Proverbs 4:5 _____

_____

_____

Characteristic _____

_____

7. Luke 15:17-20 _____

_____

_____

Characteristic _____

_____

8. 1 Corinthians 13:11 _____

_____

_____

Characteristic _____

_____

B. Christians are expected to be responsible adults. Write, in your own words, what each of the following verses says about Christians and the following three topics.

1. Being obedient to those who hold authority over you.

Romans 13:1-7 _____

_____

_____

_____

Hebrews 13:17 _____

_____

_____

_____

2. Being service minded.

Mark 10:45 _____

_____

_____

_____

Matthew 25:31-46 _____

_____

_____

_____

3. Being good Christian examples.

1 Peter 5:3 _____

_____

_____

_____

Matthew 5:13-16 _____

_____

_____

_____

II. Comprehending the Lesson

A. Give five examples of behavior you believe
   illustrate each of the following.

	Child	Immature Adult	Adult
1.	_____	_____	_____
2.	_____	_____	_____
3.	_____	_____	_____
4.	_____	_____	_____
5.	_____	_____	_____

B. What four things must you do to reach mature adulthood?

1. _____

2. _____

3. _____

4. _____

III. Writing

A. How did Adam and Eve show immaturity when God asked them what they had done?

_____

_____

_____

_____

_____

B. Select a popular figure in America and write how that person shows immaturity or maturity.

_____

_____

_____

_____

_____

_____

_____

_____

_____

C. Explain why the transition from adolescence to
    adulthood is difficult for both teens and parents.

_____

_____

_____

_____

_____

_____

_____

Intimacy

I am my beloved's, and my beloved is mine . . . .

Song of Solomon 6:3

Introduction

God placed Adam in a perfect environment in the Garden of Eden. He provided for all of Adam's physical needs. There were no such things as hurt, fear or guilt. The Creator of the universe was Adam's intimate Friend. Yet, God recognized that He had not provided Adam with all of his needs when He declared in Genesis 2:18, "It is not good that man should be alone." God had created man with needs that He would meet by forming a human relationship for Adam. He filled these needs by creating Eve and establishing the institutions of marriage and the family.

The most important quality in a great marriage is intimacy. When you are intimate with the person you love, you create unlimited possibilities for the growth of your relationship. Through intimacy, two lonely individuals can become one. Failure to bond will cause isolation and loneliness. Ultimately, it may destroy the marriage.

Guidelines for Intimacy

Intimacy requires two people and two actions, initiation and response. There must be an emotional atmosphere that will enhance intimacy and cause it to grow. You cannot independently decide to be intimate with someone. Without mutual emotional response, intimacy is non-existent.

In their book, *Secret Choices*, Dr. Ed Wheat and Gloria Okes Perkins, give ten guidelines for intimacy in marriage. They are:

- Always remember that intimacy depends on the experience of shared feelings.
- Learn by practice, to express your inner feelings to one another.
- Display mutual respect for one another, a mutual hunger to know one another better and a growing delight in one another.
- Remember that sex is no substitute for emotional intimacy.
- Fill your marriage with tender touching unrelated to sex.
- Maintain the "we" perspective.

- Communicate approval and acceptance of one another.
- Recognize and overcome fear of intimacy by building trust in actions, words and attitudes.
- Maintain the spirit of discovery in your relationship.
- Follow the pattern of Ephesians 4:22-24 in making your choices for intimacy.

Making the Guidelines Work

Emotional intimacy is the sharing of feelings. Each of the marriage partners must understand the other's feelings. You will have to learn how to talk about your inner thoughts and emotions. This may be difficult because of experiences or habits formed in childhood. Silence is the predator of intimacy: it shouts loudly, "I don't care!"

Usually women are more able to describe their emotions than men are. Often men tell the facts about a situation, never revealing how they feel emotionally. You must avoid lapsing into silence and not discussing your thoughts. Men who ask "What are you thinking?" need to be able to answer the same question honestly.

You must convince your partner that you are not indifferent to your relationship. You must listen, respond to offers, be available, be encouraging and be able to say, "I always have time for you." Never should you criticize, be too busy or have something else to do when your mate wants you near. It is easy to allow television or other distractions to substitute for intimacy. When one of the partners is in pain, the other must not be indifferent. Listen and observe to find what is causing the hurt.

Some men see pain as a sign of weakness. They do not want to acknowledge their own disconsolate feelings or console their partner's. Men often do not see the difference between sex and intimacy, while women draw a strong distinction. Hugging and kissing are immensely satisfying to women. Men, however, see those actions as precursors to sex. A good relationship requires mutual tenderness that does not always end in intercourse.

Physical contact with no sexual intent can be very emotionally satisfying. The tender stroking, holding hands or gentle hug should become private communication between the intimate husband and wife. Looks and winks that only you and your partner can interpret form an emotional bond that will help a marriage to endure.

According to counselors, couples who are experiencing problems with intimacy seldom refer to themselves as "We." The personal "I" prefaces almost every sentence. Many non-Christian counselors approve of married couples leading almost entirely separate lives, giving priority to their personal desires rather than to the common needs of the marriage. However, God's plan is for the two to become one emotionally, mentally, physically and spiritually.

Much of what we communicate to each other comes through body language, facial expressions or tone of voice. Couples must communicate approval and acceptance to each other through these avenues as well as through their words. Constantly pointing out failures or mistakes is not intimate action. Making sure your partner knows that your love is more important than his or her having forgotten to take out the garbage is one way of communicating approval.

When two people begin a marriage, they often bring with them a lack of trust in other people. Maybe they have misplaced their trust in others before and have been hurt, or they may have had families that were never open with their emotions. Whatever the reason, a lack of trust can be debilitating to a marriage. The best way to overcome lack of trust is to accept each other unconditionally, in the way that Christ accepts those who believe in Him.

Some couples believe that romance is for the dating and courtship steps of their relationship and that after the marriage they must act as a married

Bible Truths

Husbands and wives are expected to enjoy one another.

Genesis 2:23-25

Man and wife, before the entrance of sin, were entirely comfortable in the presence of one another. *25 And they were both naked, the man and his wife, and were not ashamed.*

Deuteronomy 24:5

Under the Law, God directed that a newly married couple were to spend much time together. *5 When a man has taken a new wife, he shall not go out to war or be charged with any business; he shall be free at home one year, and bring happiness to his wife whom he has taken.*

Proverbs 5:18-19

18 Let your fountain be blessed, and rejoice with the wife of your youth. 19 As a loving deer and a graceful doe, let her breasts satisfy you at all times; and be enraptured with her love.

Song of Solomon

Here is a picture of a delight of a bride and groom, or husband and wife, rightly related to one another. Several characteristics are described: their desire to be close together; their mutual feelings of unworthiness of the other's love; their desire to extol the other's virtues; their fruitful fragrant life together; their recognition of the headship of the husband; their desire to belong to one another – *My beloved is mine, and I am his* (2:16; 6:3, 10).

Ecclesiastes 9:9

Live joyfully with the wife whom you love all the days of your vain life which He has given you under the sun.

1 Corinthians 7:2-5

Marriage partners are warned against refusing to satisfy one another, except for brief times of fasting and prayer, and that by agreement.

Hebrews 13:4

Marriage is honorable among all, and the bed undefiled; but fornicators and adulterers God will judge.

Encyclopedia of Bible Truths for School Subjects
Dr. Ruth C. Haycock © ACSI

couple — whatever that is! You must keep a spirit of discovery and romance in your marriage. How is this possible with all the responsibilities of marriage and a family? One way is to "Say it with flowers." Some couples act as if every flower shop in town closed when they ended their honeymoons. You can also go away for a weekend. Where? It really does not matter. You need time to remove yourselves from everyday surroundings — to talk and go for walks. Ask your mate for a date. You can plan interesting activities around your date. Either person can ask the other and make the plans. Love notes and cards never go out of style. These intimate messages will delight your mate.

Summary

Ephesians 4:22-24 says, "that you put off, concerning your former conduct the old man which grows corrupt according to the deceitful lusts, and be renewed in the spirit of your mind, and that you put on the new man which was created according to God in true righteousness and holiness." When you follow these verses, you will stop being self-centered and selfish. As a couple, you can keep your relationship alive by studying and following God's Word. Verse 24 tells you to put on a new life that is fresh and clean in God. Marriage is a new life, just as salvation begins a new life. Put on the fresh new clothes and allow God to bless you.

One Plus One

Challenge Your Thinking

I. Bible Link

A. Read Ephesians 4:22-24. Explain how these verses illustrate a good marriage.

_____

_____

_____

_____

_____

_____

_____

_____

B. Read 1 Corinthians 11:11-12. Explain the relationship of a married couple to each other and to God.

_____

_____

_____

_____

_____

_____

_____

_____

_____

C. The Song of Solomon covers love from courtship through mature marriage. Write a paragraph for each of the six divisions of this book of the Bible.

1. The Courtship, 1:2–3:5

_____

_____

_____

_____

_____

_____

_____

2. The Procession for the Marriage, 3:6-11

_____

_____

_____

_____

_____

_____

3. The Consummation of the Marriage, 4

_____

_____

_____

_____

_____

_____

4. After the Honeymoon, 5:2–6:13

_____

_____

_____

_____

_____

_____

_____

5. The Marriage Deepens, 7:1–9:4

_____

_____

_____

_____

_____

_____

_____

6. The Maturity of Love, 8:5-14

_____

_____

_____

_____

_____

_____

II. Comprehending the Lesson

A. Write your own list of suggestions for maintaining intimacy.

1. _____

_____

2. _____

_____

3. _____

_____

4. _____

_____

5. _____

_____

6. _____

_____

7. _____

_____

8. _____

_____

9. _____

_____

10. _____

_____

B. How does Genesis 2:21–25 lay the groundwork for an intimate marriage?

_____

_____

_____

_____

_____

One Plus One

III. Writing

A. Write a paragraph describing the importance of intimacy in marriage.

_____

_____

_____

_____

_____

_____

_____

_____

B. Communication is an important component of an intimate marriage. Write a paragraph about the importance of unspoken language in an intimate relationship.

_____

_____

_____

_____

_____

_____

_____

_____

_____

_____

_____

_____

_____

_____

_____

_____

_____

_____

_____

_____

_____

_____

_____

Communication

Let no corrupt word proceed out of your mouth, but what is good for necessary edification, that it may impart grace to the hearers.

Ephesians 4:29

Introduction

In her book, *Cry Pain, Cry Hope,* Elizabeth O'Conner says that good communication is a dialogue, not a monologue. Dialogue is more than your giving time for others to say their words, and their giving time for you to say yours. A dialogue involves listening and accepting the differences you have with one another. There can be no dialogue unless we honor the differences. The purpose of a dialogue is not to persuade another person to accept our opinions, values or views. Rather, it is to create an understanding of each other and a climate in which communication takes place.

One Plus One

Maintaining good communication in a relationship is a goal toward which you must work daily. Good communication involves sending, receiving and understanding messages. Sometimes the messages are verbal. However, many times we send messages through body language and eye contact. We all communicate; our goal must be to avoid communicating poorly. How often do we experience problems because we send a poor message or misinterpret a message sent to us?

Avoiding Negatives

President Harry S Truman had a habit of writing scathing letters to those he believed had offended him. He would sit down, write the letter, and throw it in the trash can. He then would reverse the negative letter by penning one with positive solutions. When you believe you need to say something, it is a good idea to follow Truman's example. Before opening your mouth, think about what you will say. How would you want the same message delivered to you? You can apply the "Golden Rule" to your communication and speak to others as you would have them speak to you. This will help you avoid injured feelings and eliminate the need for many apologies. In Ephesians 4:29-32, Paul gives directions in communicating with others. He says to avoid corrupt communication, put away bitterness, wrath, anger and malice, and to be kind and forgiving.

An old adage is, "Silence is golden." Although this may often be true, silence can also be used as a weapon in communication. When a person retreats into silence instead of talking about problems, it leaves the other person to wonder about the severity of the issues. This is unfair to the other person and seldom leads to resolution. Everyone occasionally has his or her feelings hurt. It is childish to revert to silence or to pouting. The mature action is to openly discuss the problem and solve it. The silent treatment never leads to reconciliation. In 2 Corinthians 5:18-19, Paul teaches that Christ has given us the ministry of reconciliation. Isaiah 58:12 tells us to be repairers of broken walls.

Many couples make the mistake of trying to solve a problem after they are angry. This often becomes a shouting match with each person saying things he or she later regrets. Sometimes such conflicts lead to physical abuse. When problems erupt into anger, couples lose the ability and willingness to compromise and resolve their differences. When one partner concedes in order to quell the anger, realistic solutions are not achieved. In Ephesians 4:26, God instructs us not to let the sunset occur while we are still angry.

Negative habits of speech and listening will obstruct effective communication. Couples must avoid endless repetition, dominating conversation time and giving one-syllable answers. In Ecclesiastes 5:2-3, Solomon says that we should use few words because a fool uses a multitude of words. This does not, however, mean being short with people. You should use the number of words necessary to convey meaning. Avoiding eye contact with your partner is another way that hinders communication. This sends a subtle message of indifference to the speaker.

Scripture presents sound advice on effective communication, especially in relation to our choice of words and manner of speaking. An important principle is timing. Your position may be correct but if you choose the wrong time to approach an issue, you may lose the disagreement. Read Ecclesiastes 8:5-6 in the New International Version of the Bible.

Make sure your words meet the test of the Bible and are truthful, necessary and beneficial to the hearer.

Communication Inhibitors

Communication inhibitors are words or phrases that stop conversations rather than encourage dialogue. They are statements that hurt people's feelings and cause them to break off any further discussion. There are many types of inhibitors including:

- Commanding — "I thought I told you to return those books to the library."
- Threatening — "If you cannot remember to return the books on time, you will just have to pay the fine."

- Moralizing — "If you would just do what you were supposed to do, life would be much more pleasant."
- Criticizing — "You are always forgetting to do what you are supposed to do."
- Questioning — "Why did you forget to return those books on time?"
- Withdrawing — " It is your problem, and I do not want to hear anymore about it."
- Patronizing — "I am surprised you forgot, because you are usually so reliable and trustworthy that I don't have to worry."

Levels of Communication

We communicate on different levels to different people and in different situations. We converse one way with close friends, another way with our parents. We may speak to a stranger at a ball game, but not in the same manner as to a neighbor. In *Why Am I Afraid to Tell You Who I Am?*, John Powell says that we have five different levels of communication. These range, in reverse order, from the clichés of Level Five to the deep personal words of Level One.

Level Five in this hierarchy is *Cliché Conversation*. With little thought, we all engage in this level of conversation. We say, "How are you?" "Have a nice day." "How's the family?" There is no

Bible Truths

We must speak in a clear, appropriate manner that is understandable and listen to others as God listens to us.

Exodus 12:26-27

God said parents were to listen to their children's questions: 26 *" . . . When your children say to you, 'What do you mean by this service?' 27 That you shall say . . . ."*

Joshua 4:6-7

God directing Joshua said: 6 *" . . . That this may be a sign among you when your children ask in time to come, saying, 'What do these stones mean to you' 7 Then you shall answer them . . . . "*

Proverbs 15:1

A soft answer turns away wrath . . . .

Proverbs 15:1

A word fitly spoken is like apples of gold in settings of silver.

Proverbs 25:15

By long forbearance a ruler is persuaded, and a gentle tongue breaks a bone.

Ecclesiastes 3:1-7

1 To everything there is a season, a time for every purpose under heaven . . . . 7 . . . a time to keep silence and a time to speak.

Ecclesiastes 9:17

Words of the wise, spoken quietly should be heard rather than the shout of a ruler of fools.

John 3:1-16

Jesus listened to the questions of Nicodemus, not ignoring them as we sometimes would.

John 6:5-11

Though Jesus knew what He intended to do to feed the five thousand, He listened to Philip and Andrew and made use of the little boy's lunch, which was offered.

1 Corinthians 14:15-19

Paul expresses concern that he speak in a way that people will understand and learn.

Encyclopedia of Bible Truths for School Subjects
Dr. Ruth C. Haycock © ACSI

lengthy reply expected. Personal sharing is non-existent because we repeat these phrases without feeling any real attachment to the person.

Level Four, *Reporting Facts about Others*, requires only telling others what someone else has said. We offer no personal information in the narration. It is almost as if we are reporting the evening news.

Level Three, *My Ideas and Judgments*, leads into the beginnings of real communication. We risk relating some of our thoughts and decisions. However, if someone contradicts us or offers a stronger opinion, we will rapidly retreat to Level Four.

Level Two, *My Feelings or Emotions*, is where real sharing of feelings begins to surface. A person at this level will tell how he feels about facts, ideas and judgments.

Level One is the deepest of all communication. *Complete Emotional and Personal Communication* is absolute openness and honesty. Because this level opens the individual to the possibility of rejection of inner self, this level presents a risk factor. All married couples should strive to succeed at this level. However, success at this level may not always be continual.

Real Communication

Communication scholars have reached some interesting conclusions. A person receives 58 percent of the messages sent through the body — eye contact, facial expressions and body positions or actions. Another 35 percent of the message comes through the tone of voice. The remaining seven percent of the message is verbal. We must be aware of the messages we are sending and make sure they are clear.

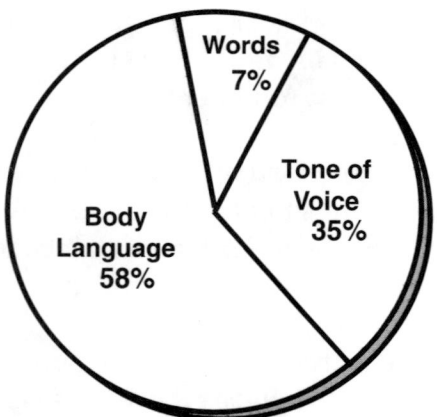

There are five key steps to genuine communication. They are:

- Listen
- Clarify and restate
- Respond
- Refocus on unity and accept that different perspectives exist.
- Resolve

You must sincerely listen when your partner is speaking. This requires your giving full attention and not just nodding your head. Do not just hear the words and tune out the message. You cannot practice selective listening, hearing only the parts you want to and ignoring the rest. Pay attention. Condition yourself to listen without dividing the time with the television or newspaper. When problems exist, an extension of this step requires the listener to ask for clarifications and to restate what has been heard. Thus, the hearer confirms that he or she has correctly understood the speaker.

Management consultants emphasize that the best way to find out how employees really think about something is to have them speak their thoughts, with the manager restating what has been said. If the employee agrees, communication takes place. This is called reflective listening. It is the same in a relationship. You must find out if you heard what your mate said. You can eliminate the need for mind reading and misinterpretation by rewording and asking for feedback.

Communication is not genuine when you attempt to say what you think your spouse wants you to say. Good communication includes clearly expressing your own thoughts. It is unfair to say, "What do you want to do tonight?" when you really want to go out to dinner. You should state your preference and not force your mate to guess.

One Plus One

It is important that your approach leads to building the relationship. There is a significant difference in the effectiveness in the following statements about the same problem.

1. You never pick up your clothes. The place looks like a pigsty!

2. I like to keep our home neat. It helps when all the clothes are put away.

The goal is to state your feelings clearly and honestly, while avoiding accusations and sarcasm. It is better to use "I" rather than "you" dictums in your statements.

There is nothing wrong with saying, "It looks like we see that differently." Couples do not have to spend their time proving one is right and the other is wrong. Communication is not a contest to be won by the best debater. Remember, women and men have different perspectives, and partners must learn to respect those differences.

There should always be a commitment to preserving the relationship. You and your mate are not opponents in a challenge match, but rather team members working out your game plan. You may disagree on strategy, but that does not lessen your determination to achieve a solution.

Summary

You cannot communicate effectively if you do not share time together. A majority of the messages we receive comes through body language. The only way to learn this language is by being close to one another. Do not let the busy life around you stop you from talking and being with your spouse.

Communication is a skill you learn by practicing. The book of Proverbs has multiple guidelines for effective communication. As a Christian, you should study the words of Solomon and learn to communicate well.

Challenge Your Thinking

I. Bible Link

A. Use the verses in Proverbs to give illustrations of the ways in which people receive communication. Write in the verses and the correct percentages.

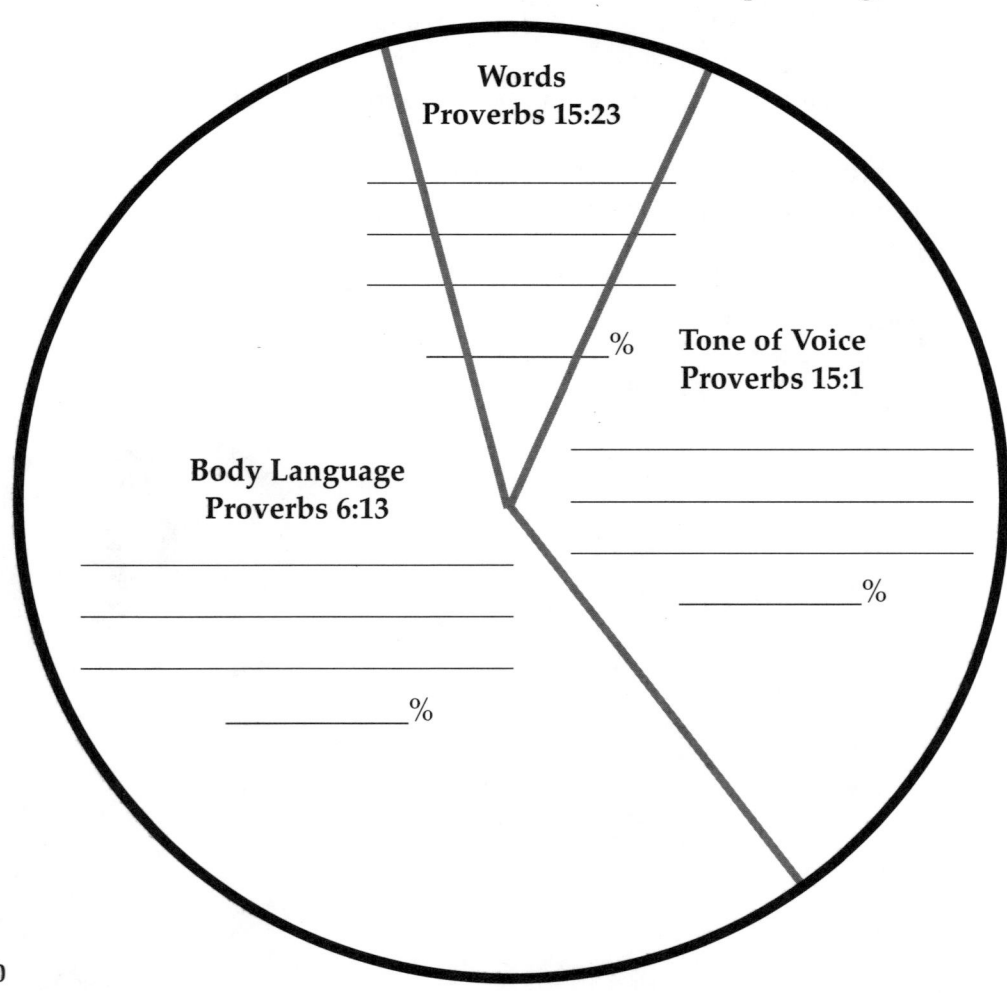

B. How do the following Proverbs illustrate
Harry S Truman's approach to letter writing?

    1. 15:28 _____

    _____

    _____

    2. 29:20 _____

    _____

    _____

    3. 26:4 _____

    _____

    _____

    4. 21:23 _____

    _____

    _____

C. One of the key steps in communication is
listening. What lesson is in the following
Proverbs?

1. 15:31 _____

_____

2. 18:13 _____

_____

3. 18:15 _____

_____

4. 19:20 _____

_____

5. 21:28 _____

_____

II. Comprehending the Lesson

A. Define, in your own words, the following two words relating to good communications.

1. monologue _____

_____

2. dialogue _____

_____

B. List five negatives to be avoided in good communication.

1. _____

2. _____

3. _____

4. _____

5. _____

One Plus One

III. Writing

A. Write down a situation in which someone failed to do something you expected of them. Then, using the communication inhibitors, write responses to the situation.

Expectation: _____

1. Commanding: _____

_____

2. Threatening: _____

_____

3. Moralizing: _____

_____

4. Criticizing: _____

_____

5. Questioning: _____

_____

6. Withdrawing: _____

_____

B. Based on Proverbs 15:1, 4; 16:1 and 25:15, write
   a positive response to the expectation in III.A.

   _____

   _____

   _____

   _____

   _____

   _____

   _____

   _____

10

Roles and Responsibilities

Submitting to one another in the fear of God.

Ephesians 5:21

Introduction

The July 1986 issue of *Reader's Digest* contained a story of a little boy lost in a supermarket. A helpful worker came to his rescue and led him through the aisles looking for his mother. She kept asking him, "Do you see your mother?" The boy kept replying "No!" as they went from aisle to aisle. Finally, she stood him on a counter at the front of the store and asked the question once more. This time he replied, "No, I just keep seeing my daddy." The child answered the only question put to him. It was the clerk who thought the mother would be doing the shopping.

Society presupposes some roles for husbands and wives that may or may not be Biblical. Where society and the world may be confused, the Bible is clear about the primary roles and relationships of husbands and wives in the Christian home. God has outlined the principles of husbands and wives within the family in an uncomplicated manner.

Biblical Principles

Society often misrepresents the Bible concerning men and women by declaring the Bible as a "sexist" book. It is important to understand what the Bible teaches about the roles of males and females.

Genesis 1:26-28 teaches that God created both man and woman in His image. Each had a direct relationship with God and shared jointly the responsibilities of rearing children. They also had joint dominion over God's created order on Earth and joint responsibility in establishing families and society. When God formed woman from man, He demonstrated the fundamental unity and equality of human beings. The word "suitable" in Genesis 2:18 denotes equality and fitting to needs.

Jesus Christ came to redeem women as well as men. We all become children of God, one in Christ, and heirs to the blessings of salvation, without reference to gender distinctions (Galatians 3:26–29). God calls both women and men to develop their spiritual gifts in 1 Peter 4:10-11 and to use these gifts as stewards of the grace of God.

Husbands and wives are heirs together of the grace of life. They bind together in a relationship of mutual submission and responsibility. In Ephesians 5:21, Colossians 3:19 and 1 Peter 3:7, the Bible gives the husband's role as head of the family. His role is not to dominate. He must be self-giving, loving and serving in a mutually submissive relationship.

These Biblical principles have practical application in the Christian home. Husband and wife are to defer to each other in seeking to fulfill each other's needs, desires and aspirations. Neither spouse is to seek to dominate the other. Each is to act as a humble servant of the other. It is not always a question of who will make certain decisions, but which one is better able to do so. It is upon this framework of Biblical equality that the roles of husbands and wives are to function.

Husbands

It is interesting that in describing the responsibilities of the husband and father, the Bible uses action verbs. Husbands are to do things, not just react to situations.

Colossians 3:19 is a clear statement of the relationship of a husband to his wife. Paul says, "Husbands love your wives and do not be bitter against them." The man's first duty toward his wife is to love her. There are no qualifications or limitations placed on this. The second part of the verse,

"do not be bitter," can be translated as, "do not be harsh." This focuses on the man's attitude toward his wife. He manifests his love by a conscious decision to devote himself to his wife and always seek her highest well-being. This is the Biblical love that a husband should show his wife. Ephesians 5:25 tells how the husband's relationship to his wife is the same as Christ's relationship to the church. Here husbands receive the instruction, "Husbands love your wives, just as Christ also loved the church, and gave Himself for her."

The husband's leadership forms the core of the Christian home. In 1 Corinthians 11:3, Paul says, "But I want you to know that the head of every man is Christ, the head of woman is man, and the head of Christ is God." Many people misinterpret this verse to somehow place women in an inferior position. The Bible does not teach that women are inferior, but that men should exercise leadership within the family.

A husband's leadership extends to spiritual matters. As the spiritual leader in the home, the husband is to regularly study the Word of God and pray so that he can properly minister to the family's spiritual needs. As the head, the husband leads as the couple evaluate the marriage and achieve mutual goals.

According to 1 Timothy 5:8, the husband is responsible for providing for his family. Paul wrote to Timothy, "But if anyone does not provide for his own, and especially for those of his household, he has denied the faith and is worse than an unbeliever." A husband's failure to provide for his family makes him worse than an unbeliever. When a man accepts the benefits and responsibilities of marriage, he assumes the responsibility of providing for the physical, financial and security needs of his family.

Wives

Today's society has blurred the distinction between the roles of women and men in marriage. Ephesians 5:21-33 and Proverbs 31 illustrate a wife's role and responsibilities. These verses do not mean that a woman is inferior nor do they limit or burden her. The focus of Ephesians 5:22, "Wives, submit to your own husbands, as to the Lord," is on the function or role of wives in a loving relationship.

Proverbs 31:25-28 show the strength and honor a woman has in marriage:

> *Strength and honor are her clothing;*
> *She shall rejoice in time to come.*
> *She opens her mouth with wisdom,*
> *And on her tongue is the law of kindness.*
> *She watches over the ways of her household,*
> *And does not eat the bread of idleness,*
> *Her children rise up and call her blessed;*
> *Her husband also, and he praises her.*

Bible Truths

The headship of the home belongs to the husband and father.

Genesis 2:20-23

God made man before woman; He made woman to prevent loneliness and provide human fellowship for Adam. Also it was to Adam God spoke when he found them hiding in the garden; He held Adam accountable.

Genesis 3:16

As a result of man's sin, God pronounced that the husband would rule over the wife.

1 Peter 3:7

. . . Likewise you husbands, dwell with them with understanding, giving honor to the wife, as to the weaker vessel, and as being heirs together of the grace of life, that your prayers may not be hindered.

Genesis 3:16

God spoke specifically to Eve, saying: *16 . . . Your desire shall be for your husband, and he shall rule over you.*

Ephesians 5:21-33

Mutual submission is to characterize believers in many relationships, as shown in these verses. In particular wives are told: *22 Submit to your own husbands, as to the Lord. 23 For the husband is head of the wife, as also Christ is head of the church; and He is the Savior of the body. 24 Therefore just as the church is subject to Christ, so let wives be to their own husbands in everything. 33 The wife see that she respects her husband.*

1 Peter 3:1

Likewise you wives, be submissive to your own husbands, that even if some do not obey the word, they, without a word, may be won by the conduct of their wives.

Encyclopedia of Bible Truths for School Subjects
Dr. Ruth C. Haycock © ACSI

A Christian wife provides the stability in a home and makes daily decisions on how to run the household. She does this in the context of loving her husband as Christ loves her.

Mutual Submission

In *Christian: Celebrate Your Sexuality*, Dwight H. Small says, "When a man and woman unite in marriage, humanity experiences a restoration to wholeness. The glory of the man is the acknowledgment that woman was created for him; the glory of the woman is the acknowledgment that man was incomplete without her. The humility of the woman is the acknowledgment that she was made for man; the humility of man is the acknowledgment that he is incomplete without her. Both share an equal dignity, honor and worth. Yes, and each shares a humility before the other, also."

Mutual submissiveness in marriage is similar to the submissiveness in the relationship between believers in the body of Christ. A person with a particular spiritual gift may exercise leadership at a certain time. However, that does not mean that person leads all the time. The leader is always Jesus Christ. In a marriage, the leadership in a mutually submissive relationship is determined by a joint decision by the partners. Capability, not gender, should determine who has responsibility for various areas of decision making. Ultimately all decisions are to be based on the leadership of Jesus Christ.

One Plus One

Authority Structure

All of life involves various roles assigned within authority structures. These involve obedience and submission to those in authority:

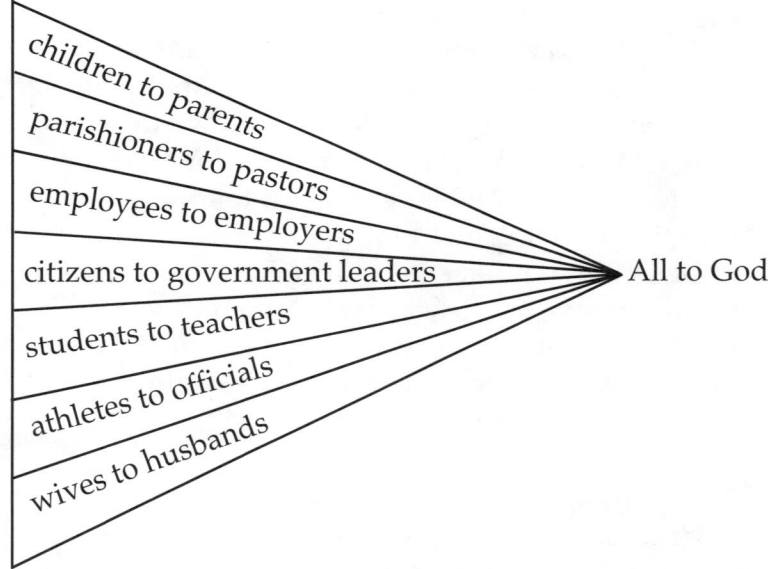

Scripture directs those in authority not to "lord it over" others. At the same time, we are to be in submission to those in authority over us. This is especially true of wives and husbands according to 1 Peter 3. In every organization, there must be a final voice of decision, a place where "the buck stops here." In a home, this responsibility belongs to the husband. There are times, even in disagreement, when a wife must lovingly submit to her husband. This requires her to place greater confidence in the Lord to work through her husband to accomplish what is best for the family.

Summary

A godly family is a microcosm of the relationship between Christ and the church. It provides an example of real love. According to John 13:34, it is through love that the world will know we are His disciples.

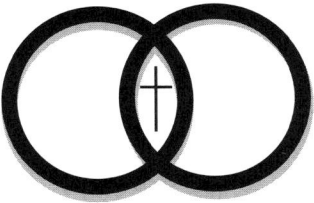

One Plus One

Challenge Your Thinking

I. Bible Link

A. Use the following verses to describe what the Old Testament says about the roles and responsibilities of husbands and wives.

1. Proverbs 31

_____

_____

_____

2. 1 Kings 16:29 and 22:40

_____

_____

_____

3. Genesis 11:27 and 23:3

_____

_____

_____

B. Use the following verses to describe what the
   New Testament says about the roles and
   responsibilities of husbands and wives.

    1. Ephesians 5

      _____

      _____

      _____

    2. Colossians 3

      _____

      _____

      _____

    3. Titus 2:3-5

      _____

      _____

      _____

    4. 1 Peter 3:7

      _____

      _____

      _____

5. 1 Corinthians 7:3-5

_____

_____

_____

II. Comprehending the Lesson

A. Circle the appropriate numeral to indicate the answer that most closely reflects your beliefs: 1=Strongly Agree; 2=Somewhat Agree; 3=Not Sure; 4=Somewhat Disagree; 5=Strongly Disagree.

1. The husband should be the head of the home.
   1   2   3   4   5

2. The wife's primary responsibility is to manage the home and care for the children.
   1   2   3   4   5

3. When spouses cannot agree, the husband should make the final decision.
   1   2   3   4   5

4. The wife should always do what the husband says to do.
   1   2   3   4   5

5. A mother should never take a job that will take her out of the home.
   1   2   3   4   5

6. It is a good idea for husbands and wives to take separate vacations.
   1   2   3   4   5

7. The primary responsibility for disciplining the children belongs to the father.
   1   2   3   4   5

8. Husbands should never do household chores.
   1   2   3   4   5

9. The relationship between husband and wife should be based on mutual submission.
   1   2   3   4   5

10. A husband should have a night out with his friends without his wife knowing the details.
    1   2   3   4   5

11. A wife should keep any money she earns for herself.
    1   2   3   4   5

12. A wife should cook and the husband should cut the grass.
    1   2   3   4   5

13. A couple should have a special date together once a month.
    1   2   3   4   5

14. The husband should make all financial decisions and manage all money.
    1   2   3   4   5

One Plus One

B. List five things that society has stereotyped as the roles for husbands and wives.

1. _____ _____

2. _____ _____

3. _____ _____

4. _____ _____

5. _____ _____

III. Writing

A. Describe how the relationship of a husband and wife is similar to that of Jesus to the church.

_____

_____

_____

_____

_____

_____

B. Describe the humility a husband and wife
    should have toward each other.

    1. The humility of the wife is _____

    _____

    2. The humility of the husband is _____

    _____

C. Describe what you believe your role would be in
    a marriage relationship. _____

    _____

    _____

    _____

    _____

    _____

    _____

Unit Three

Marriage and Family

*Your wife shall be as a fruitful vine in the
very heart of your house; your children like olive
plants all around your table. Behold, thus shall the
man be blessed who fears the LORD.*

Psalm 128:3–4

The *Los Angeles Times* newspaper asked
2,000 adults, "What is your main goal in life?"
The most overwhelming-given response
was, ". . . to be happily married." This
should not be surprising. Census figures
show that over 90 percent of the people in the
United States will marry at least one time in their
lives. Marriage is one of the most durable institutions on earth and has incredible potential for
happiness.

The family, with its cornerstone of marriage, is
the basic societal institution for stability in a nation.
This makes it imperative that Christian couples

understand the responsibilities of marriage and parenthood. The world often denigrates marriage, but Christians know that it is an institution created by God that holds our society together.

You must approach the step of marriage and family in a realistic manner. Everything is not all sunshine and roses. There will be stresses and problems. Your duty as a Christian is to overcome these and become a light to a world that, today, accepts the breakdown of marriages and families as the norm. As a couple, you must compromise differences before they become irreconcilable.

You need to understand the things that erode and weaken marriage so that you can help reverse the increase in disrupted marriages. One of the main causes of weak marriages is the lack of strong Christian faith and family worship. Without family worship and regular church attendance as a firm foundation, families have difficulty overcoming the strains the world places on them.

Couples do not enter a marriage with the idea of not succeeding. Almost all believe in "happily ever after" and think their marriage is the perfect one. When a marriage fails, it disrupts not only the couple, but untold numbers of others. Christians need to do everything they can to succeed.

The step of marriage and family in your life will be filled with high points and low points. It is up to you to enjoy the high points and overcome the low points. We will look at marriage and the family from several different perspectives. First will be the importance of worship. Second is how to be financially responsible. Third, we will discuss the extended family and daily living. Fourth is the joys and challenges of children. The last chapter gives testimony to marriages that endure.

11

Family Worship

But as for me, and my house, we will serve the LORD.

Joshua 24: 15

Introduction

The way in which a couple perceives religion and worship is the cornerstone of a marriage. When two people come together, they bring with them all their knowledge, training and faith. Much of their religious background comes from their respective families. Each must discuss and understand the other's background before they begin marriage.

In their book, *Getting Ready for Marriage*, Jerry D. Hardin and Dianne C. Sloane state, "Religion has a deeper family interconnection than any other topic . . . ." They point out the need for understanding the importance of God in a family relationship and how each spouse, and later the children, work together in this understanding.

One Plus One

"In the Scriptures, Jesus spoke about how His relationship to His people is like a marriage. That relationship is special, a covenant, in fact, a oneness. This oneness, this compatibility, is only achieved when you share the same basic beliefs. These are the very foundation of your marriage relationship. From this foundation come the building blocks of how you conduct yourselves, your moral standards, values, and ethics."

Establishing a Base

You and your spouse will have answered most of the basic questions about worship in premarital counseling and private conversations before the marriage. If not, you must do so early in your life together. Hardin and Sloane pose questions that a couple should consider.

- How compatible are you in your religious beliefs?
- How do you see God?
- Who is God?
- Is Jesus Christ your personal Savior?
- Will you, as a couple, go to church?
- Which church?
- How involved will you be in the church?
- When and how do you believe a person should be baptized?

These are only a few of the questions, which you need to answer. The two of you will need to develop a home worship culture, in which you answer additional questions.

- Will there be prayer before bedtime?
- What about prayer at every mealtime?
- Does this include restaurants?
- What are valid reasons for missing church?
- Will there be daily Bible reading?
- What about morning worship time?
- Who will be responsible for leading family worship?

In Deuteronomy 6:4-7, Moses presents the home as the central place of spiritual teaching and learning. His statements provide the basis for answering questions about worship.

Hear, O Israel: The LORD our God, the LORD is one!

You shalt love the LORD thy God with all your heart, with all your soul, and with all your strength.

And these words which I command you today, shall be in your heart.

You shall teach them diligently to your children, and shall talk of them when you sit in your house, and when you walk by the way, when you lie down, and when you rise up.

One Plus One

Principles for Positive Family Worship

The Bible provides guidelines for family worship, but it does not dictate exact procedures. God allows a Christian family the opportunity to define the way in which it will conduct worship in each home. This worship style will develop from individual backgrounds, the church you are attending and your family needs. However, the plan of worship should follow principles that will create a positive experience for all family members. Your worship should be flexible, practical, varied, inclusive and natural.

Many families fall into the trap of "authoritarianism" and lack flexibility in their family worship. They maintain a style or schedule that they will not alter for any reason. You should not allow family worship to become an exercise in legalism in which your children or spouse believe that God will somehow love them less if they miss one day of a particular worship. "No Bible — No breakfast," may be easy to remember but unrealistic on mornings when you are rushing or an unforeseen event occurs. You can always substitute a prayer and ask for circumstances to change tomorrow. As schedules change, the family should alter worship times.

Your flexibility extends to prayers at mealtime. These prayers do not always have to be so similar that they become repetitive. Chuck Swindoll said, "Why not just talk to God?" Prayer does not always have to be a formal presentation of "Thank yous" and "Wants." Pa Kettle, in the book and movie *The Egg and I*, gave a brief and effective family worship prayer. Ma and Pa Kettle had 13 children. As they rushed to the dinner table and took their seats, Pa raised his hat, they all bowed their heads and Pa said, " 'preciate it . . . !" There was no long oratory; yet the prayer covered the issue and was acceptable worship.

Practicality is important, especially after there are children. Mom and Dad may find interest in lofty discussions of theology. These may be impractical for their children. The more children talk during family worship, the more parents can understand the problems the children have. Parents can then discuss these problems by using God's Word to address the problems. The subject matter of books, discussions and activities must be age-appropriate for all members of the family. Children will not learn from materials too advanced or irrelevant to their lives.

Families should not go through the motions of worship just to fill a prearranged time or idea. This does not produce true family worship. Family worship should fit the needs of each member of the family.

Variety is probably the one principle that Christian families usually exclude from worship time. Worship, in too many Christian homes, is a

Bible Truths

Right attitude toward God results in right family relationships.

Leviticus 19:2-3

Showing proper respect for parents is part of being set apart for God. *2 . . . You shall be holy, for I the LORD your God am holy. 3 Every one of you shall revere his mother and his father and keep My Sabbaths . . . .*

Psalm 128:1-6

1 Blessed is every one who fears the LORD, who walks in His ways . . . . 3 Your wife shall be like a fruitful vine in the very heart of your house, your children like olive plants all around your table. . . . 6 Yes, may you see your children's children. Peace be upon Israel.

Acts 16:30-34

When the Philippian jailer believed on Christ, he and his family ministered to the physical needs of Paul and Silas. There was oneness in the family.

Genesis 39:5

Joseph was a slave in Potiphar's house, yet he brought blessing. *5 . . . the LORD blessed the Egyptian's house for Joseph's sake; and the blessing of the LORD was on all that he had in the house and in the field.*

Exodus 18:9-12

As Jethro, a Midianite priest, observed his son-in-law Moses, he was convinced of the sovereignty and power of God.

1 Corinthians 7:13-14

In a divided household, where the wife is a believer and the husband an unbeliever, the woman is told not to leave him, because *14 the unbelieving husband is sanctified by the wife.* Also it is said of the children, *. . . Now they are holy.*

1 Peter 3:1

Wives are commanded to be in subjection to their own husbands so that *1 . . . if some do not obey the word, they, without a word, may be won by the conduct of their wives.*

Encyclopedia of Bible Truths for
School Subjects
Dr. Ruth C. Haycock © ACSI

meaningless routine, doing the same thing, in the same way, at the same time every day. Children and adults like to have different experiences and approach worship activities in different ways.

Family worship can include singing, reading Christian books, walking, talking and discussing God's Creation. A beautiful sunset may become a part of family worship. You do not always have to sit in a group and read verses from the Bible. Families can also break into age or gender groups to discuss issues of faith.

Several Christian organizations have videos and recordings of adventures for young people. The family can use these for family worship and discussions about moral choices. Families on vacation can stop at a highway rest area to give thanks to God. Couples and families can attend retreats and seminars. Families must use their imaginations to develop invigorating and exciting worship of God.

It is important to include the whole family in worship time. Dad should not always lead the worship as if he were the pastor, even if he is! As often as possible, each family member should have the opportunity to lead some part of the family worship. Allow the person who plays the piano to play some hymns. Have the youngest member of the family tell about the Sunday school lesson. The teenagers may want to relate what has happened in church youth department.

As Deuteronomy implies, family worship should not be something extraordinary. It should be routine in the Christian home. When worship is part of the fabric of their lives, children and parents naturally give time to God. God becomes an integral part of their day. It is not as if a part of their day is merely being donated to God. Natural family worship allows Jesus to function as a member of the family. A Christian family sees God's handiwork in everything and gives Him praise.

Planning and Preparation

You cannot expect effective family worship to occur automatically. It takes planning and preparation. Part of the preparation is to begin worshiping together early in your relationship. Reach an agreement about fundamental questions of faith and beliefs. Investigate your spiritual gifts, and as Paul says in 1 Timothy 4:14, "Do not neglect the gift that is in you . . . ." One of you may sing in the choir. The other may teach Sunday School. Each of you must be active in your local church.

Set aside time in your busy lives to worship. This includes Sunday services, Bible studies and other church activities. Learn how to have family worship at home. Plan specific times for home worship. The worship schedule should neither enslave you nor be broken without good reason. When you have children, they will see what is most important in your life.

Family Worship

The world offers many attractive activities that lure Christians away or make them resent family and church worship. Your 14-year-old resents missing his favorite television program. The 17-year old complains she cannot spare the time for worship because of school assignments. A basketball game on Wednesday night appears more enticing than church service. Choir practice interferes with a couple's quality time. Your six-year-old thinks it is cute to refuse to say grace at mealtime. All of these can cause family worship time to become a battleground.

You can avoid conflict by planning and preparing times for worship but you must remember the principles of family worship. Do not schedule a worship time that will cause a problem with school work. Yet do not let school work interfere on a regular basis. You can use homework as a time to pray for guidance in accomplishing the task. If one spouse is in the choir, the other can attend the practices or use the time to talk with their children. Do not ignore a child's interest in television. Take time to watch programs with him or her and discuss how they are appropriate for Christians, or how the subject matter offends God. Be prepared to help other family members resist the temptations of the world. Family worship is the time to accomplish this.

One Plus One

Summary

Make family worship a time of joy. It is for giving praise to the Lord and learning about His positive influence on your family. There is a saying, "The family that prays together stays together." In your family worship, you can bring to God all the issues affecting your lives. You need to bring problems, accomplishments, illness, health, homework, entertainment, friends, enemies and praises to Him. As God answers prayer in your family, it cements the relationship you all share with Him.

Family Worship

Challenge Your Thinking

I. Bible Link

A. What effect should the following verses have on family worship?

    1. Amos 3:3 _____

    _____

    2. 2 Corinthians 6:14 _____

    _____

    3. Joshua 24:15 _____

    _____

B. How do Moses' words in Deuteronomy 6:4-7 set a pattern for home worship?

_____

_____

_____

_____

_____

One Plus One

II. **Comprehending the Lesson**

A. How does family worship bond relationships together?

_____

_____

_____

_____

_____

B. Give three examples each of how a family can meet the five principles of family worship.

1. Flexible _____

_____

_____

2. Practical _____

_____

_____

3. Varied _____

_____

_____

4. Inclusive _____

_____

_____

5. Natural _____

_____

_____

C. Check the appropriate box to indicate your answer to the following questions related to family worship.

Yes/No

❏　❏　1. Should family members pray before bedtime?

❏　❏　2. Should families pray at every mealtime?

❏　❏　3. Is it proper to pray aloud in restaurants?

❏　❏　4. Are there valid reasons for missing church?

❏　❏　5. Should there be scheduled Bible reading time?

III. Writing

A. Write two paragraphs describing your ideas of how to develop a home worship culture.

_____

_____

_____

_____

_____

_____

_____

_____

_____

_____

B. Plan and schedule an ideal family worship plan for your prospective family.

1. Sunday _____

_____

_____

2. Monday _____

_____

_____

3. Tuesday _____

_____

_____

4. Wednesday _____

_____

_____

5. Thursday _____

_____

_____

6. Friday _____

   _____

   _____

7. Saturday _____

   _____

   _____

12

Financial Responsibility

His Lord said unto him, Well done, good and faithful servant; you were faithful over a few things, I will make you ruler over many things. Enter into the joy of your Lord.

Matthew 25: 21

Introduction

The materialistic mind-set of today's society causes a major financial problem for newlyweds. Because of peer pressure, many young couples try to acquire too much, too soon. Consequently, what they may acquire is enormous debt. This debt causes financial pressures and leads to friction between the couple.

How important is money? Jesus spoke more about money than any other subject. He dedicated many of His parables to teaching the principles of how to handle money properly. Jesus draws a clear parallel between the way we handle money and the manner in which we respond to spiritual matters. The way we handle our finances is a good indicator of what we truly value.

Christians need to be responsible in all aspects of their lives, but they must pay particular attention to their finances. It is easy to creep into debt. A young person will go into debt because of a college loan. After graduation, he is surprised to learn that he owes more than $10,000. When marriage doubles the indebtedness, trouble can ensue. Another insidious debt creator is when credit card companies send unsolicited credit cards to college students, who readily enter the "easy money" culture. New cars, expensive apartments, dining out, fine furniture and other costly purchases can create mayhem in marriages.

Later, when a couple has children, they can incur debt above their ability to pay. Modern society can decree clothing styles and other expensive items, the desire for which cause a family to lose sight of fiscal responsibility. God wants His children to be happy, but He also wants them to be good stewards of the things He allows them to have.

Fundamental Financial Responsibility

God has given four practical financial principles that will help in marital life. You should follow these principles when listening to advice from family, friends, marriage counselors and your pastor. First

Timothy 6:7 acknowledges that God has complete ownership of your resources. Luke 14:28 directs us to plan expenditures. Proverbs 24:3-4 advises us to maintain accurate and complete records. Proverbs 14:15 encourages us to learn more about fiscal matters.

Paul told Timothy, "For we brought nothing into this world, and it is certain we can carry nothing out." Once you accept the concept that God owns everything, you will manage all of your assets according to His will. You are to be a good steward of what God has allowed you to have.

Jesus said in the Gospel of Luke, "For which of you, intending to build a tower, does not sit down first and count the cost, whether he has enough to finish it." Failure to plan financial expenditures is one of the greatest problems married couples face. Planning includes establishing an annual budget, when and where to make major purchases, and establishing a cache for emergencies.

Solomon wrote in Proverbs, "Through wisdom a house is built, and by understanding it is established; by knowledge the rooms are filled with all precious and pleasant riches." It is impossible to control your spending if you do not have a clear idea of the amount you are spending and what items are being purchased. Without current, complete financial records, you will never know whether or not you can save for the down payment on a house, purchase a car or afford a baby.

Bible Truths

Money is entrusted to believers for use as God purposes.

Three uses for money seem to be especially emphasized in Scripture: (1) the care of one's family, (2) the needs of others (3) the furtherance of the Gospel.

Mark 7:9-13

Jesus, rebuking the Pharisees, says: *11 But you say, 'if a man says to his father or mother, "Whatever profit you might have received from me is Corban (that is, dedicated to the temple) 12 and you no longer let him do anything for his father or his mother; 13 you make the word of God of no effect.*

1 Timothy 5:8

But if anyone does not provide for his own, and especially for those of his household, he has denied the faith and is worse than an unbeliever.

Deuteronomy 15:10-11

10 You shall surely give to him, and your heart should not be grieved when you give him, because for this thing the LORD your God will bless you in all your works and in all to which you put your hand. 11 For the poor will never cease from the land; therefore I command you, saying, 'You shall open your hand wide to your brother, to your poor and your needy, in your land.'

Ephesians 4:28

Let him who stole steal no longer, but rather let him labor, working with his hands what is good, that he may have something to give him who has need.

Genesis 14:20

Before the Law was given, Abraham gave tithes of all that he gained in battle. He have them to Melchizedek, recognizing him as a representative of God.

Leviticus 27:30-34

The details of the tithe for Israel are given here: *30 And all the tithe of the land, whether of the seed of the land or of the fruit of the tree, is the Lord's . It is holy to the LORD.*

Encyclopedia of Bible Truths for School Subjects
Dr. Ruth C. Haycock © ACSI

Financial Responsibility

Most newlywed couples lack financial wisdom and need to increase their financial knowledge. Solomon says, "The simple believes every word, but the prudent considers well his steps." Prudent couples need to know:

- How to balance a checkbook
- How to figure the actual interest rate on credit purchases
- How much money should be saved for emergencies
- How to figure the tax liability at the end of a year
- How to establish a workable budget

"Danger! Handle with Care!"

Larry Burkett, president of Christian Financial Concepts, says that the first advice he gives to young couples is about credit and how it can destroy a family. Credit itself is not the problem; the misuse is. Burkett believes couples should label all credit cards with the warning, "Danger! Handle with Care!"

Many young couples begin their descent into debt even before marriage. The ease of obtaining credit helps to create an illusion of financial security. Credit card companies send unsolicited credit cards to college students, who will charge the cost of a pizza on a credit card and pay an 18 percent annual interest rate. If a couple has a $2,500 balance on a credit card, makes no more charges, but pays the minimum payment, they will need 30 years to pay off the total at an 18 percent interest rate.

Some couples begin soon after the wedding ceremony to buy things without regard for the financial implications. They borrow to buy a new car, have nice furniture and to take a vacation. Couples soon become so deeply in debt that they often consolidate their debts. The trouble is that most of them will not change their spending habits and will accumulate both the consolidated debt and the new debt. Burkett says that this occurs more often than most people believe, and that debt is the basic disagreement in 80 percent of divorces.

Joint Sharing

Couples handle money in different ways. Some have separate bank accounts and are individually responsible for the way the money is used, without accountability to the partner. Some husbands control the funds entirely, often not even disclosing their salaries to their wives. Instead, the wife receives a weekly allowance and has to pay all household and personal expenses from that money. If she uses all of her allowance, she either does without or has to ask for additional money from her husband. This is often humiliating. Many women in this situation secretly build up funds for themselves.

Most couples share financial responsibility. Both partners know all the assets and debts and work together to establish a budget. Couples need to discuss finances and be comfortable in making joint decisions. One cannot blame the other for causing debt; it has to be a partnership.

When preparing to establish a budget, Burkett says that couples make three mistakes that must be avoided. First, some husbands try to use a budget to attack their wives' spending, which they often misunderstand. Second, they create an unrealistic budget that has no chance of being successful. Third, couples believe that a budget will immediately solve their bad spending habits. Budgets should be annual. They will sometimes take a year to achieve stability and successful implementation.

Preparing to Budget

Young couples become discouraged with annual budgets because many model plans require a larger income than they have. Financial planners give guidelines concerning percentages, which should apply to categories of expenditures. These percentages will vary according to a family's priorities and preferences. Couples must begin with their income and prepare a spending plan based on that amount. Their basic plan defines the way in which the money will be spent.

One Plus One

A major part of the budget-making process is determining who will be treasurer. In his book, *Getting Ready for Marriage*, David R. Mace states, "Some couples decide who will manage the money on the basis of who is better equipped for this task, regardless of sex." Larry Burkett recommends that the wife handle the bookkeeping. "She is typically more disciplined and more motivated to make the budget succeed." The important thing is to discuss the way in which the family will handle the finances. If the couple decides to have separate checking accounts, it is imperative that the couple knows who is responsible for paying each of the bills.

When creating a budget, it is a good idea to begin with a hypothetical one. The preferred time to do this is during the courtship and engagement steps. It should be no later than the first few months of marriage. A couple working on a hypothetical budget will reveal their basic attitudes toward money management.

Mace advises the couple to "[Estimate] as nearly as you can what your joint income might be. Then make estimates as accurately as you can of all the basic expenditures that would come out of this income: housing, utilities, furnishings, food, clothes, medical care, continuing education, personal items, automobile, vacation, insurance, savings, charities and the like." You then can see how to live within the income. This is not to be an actual budget. It will serve as an opening for discussions of areas of agreement and disagreement.

Creating a Budget

In order to achieve a workable annual budget, couples need to communicate effectively. Once they open their discussion, they will readily find which major categories are most important to them, and what percentages of the income will apply to each category. Except for two categories, Christian couples can vary the percentages to fit their lifestyle. The two exceptions are: a tithe to their church and a percentage for taxes.

After the two amounts above are subtracted, the remainder can be considered as 100 percent of usable income. If the gross income is $25,000, and the tithe and taxes are estimated to total $6,250, it leaves a spendable income of $18,750. This amount should be divided into categories. Young couples must realize that their gross income is not the amount they can spend during the year.

Larry Burkett suggests the following categories and percentages and emphasizes that these are guidelines. However, once a couple establishes the annual categories and percentages, they must follow through for the year. Slight alterations can be allowed. Major reallocations should be delayed until the following year.

One Plus One

Housing = 36%
Rent/Mortgage
Utilities
Property taxes
Repairs/Upkeep
Furnishings

Transportation = 16%
Car Loan
Fuel/Fares
Repairs
Insurance

Food = 22%
Groceries
Restaurants

Entertainment = 8%
Recreation
Vacations

Insurance = 5%
Health/Medical
Life

Clothing = 5%
Work/Leisure
Cleaning

Savings = 5%

Miscellaneous = 3%
Celebrations/Gifts
Medical Care Items
Personal Care Items

A couple with $18,750 after tithes and taxes would have approximately $1,562 monthly to allocate for expenditures. Following the above percentages, their allotted expenses would be:

- housing $562
- food $343
- automobile $250
- entertainment $125
- insurance $ 78
- clothes $ 78
- savings $ 78
- miscellaneous $ 47

Budget Breakers

The majority of families in the United States today are two-income families. Young couples, in particular, must be aware that a wife's income can both benefit and hurt. The additional income provides for a more flexible budget. It also increases the ability to borrow money. If a couple becomes accustomed to living on the wife's income and decide to have a child, they may need to borrow in order to maintain their standard of living. Dependency upon her income may prevent her being home to care for the children.

Responsibilities of dual careers add significant stress. Managing the home, caring for children, participating in church, building the marriage relationship and daily activities become more difficult. It is wise for a couple to limit spending and allow the wife to remain at home or expect to work only if and when:

- There are no children in the home.
- There is a short-term goal, such as saving for a down payment on a home or paying off debts.
- There is sufficient help available in the home to eliminate the additional stress.
- There are absolutely no other choices.

One Plus One

Many young people become "insurance poor" by having more insurance than is necessary. Young couples need to buy insurance which will allow the family to maintain an adequate level of living, should the main income provider die. However, many advisors warn against over-purchasing insurance plans.

Couples need to be extremely careful about impulse buying. This type of buying destroys a budget. Television situation comedies stereotype women as the impulsive buyers. However, most families sink into debt because of the husbands' impulsive purchases. Women buy extra food items for the home and too many clothes, but men buy utility vehicles, jet skis and big-screen televisions on impulse. Spouses should consult one another before making unbudgeted purchases.

Impulse buying is aided by the easy-credit mystique of credit cards. Often the amount of interest consumes a high percentage of a family's income. Couples must learn to control the use of this increasingly prevalent"plastic money." Many of your grandparents would buy things only when they could pay cash. It was disgraceful to be in debt. Most young couples find that attitude toward debt and buying unrealistic. Yet they can learn to control credit. If not, they will increase the possibility of facing major marital difficulties.

Savings?

Should your budget include savings? The standard answer is yes. However, many young couples find it difficult to save money. Even when they do have money to place in savings, it is difficult to know the best place to invest. Larry Burkett says, "If you want my advice about investments, don't take my advice." He says he knows what works for him, but it will not necessarily work for others.

Family advisors suggest that a family have a four-month income reserve in emergency savings. This can be used in case of job loss, illness, natural disaster and other short-term emergency.

Other savings should be designated so that the couple will realize its importance. David Mace says that major savings should provide for three things: down payment for a house, education of children and retirement. Most people will never save enough to be wealthy, but some type of investment will make life more stable.

Summary

Christian couples and families are obligated to sound financial management. This is true whether you have a great deal of money or very little. By following God's principles, you will be able to be comfortable with what He has given you.

One Plus One

Challenge Your Thinking

I. Bible Link

    A. Write the financial principle that fits the Bible verse.

        1. Proverbs 14:15

_____

_____

        2. Proverbs 24:3-4

_____

_____

        3. Luke 14:28

_____

_____

        4. 1 Timothy 6:7

_____

_____

    B. What advice does Matthew 25:21 give you about finances?

_____

_____

_____

_____

C. Use a Bible concordance to find and list five references pertaining to tithing and giving to the Lord.

_____

_____

_____

_____

_____

D. After studying the verses in C, list the principles that should govern tithes and gifts to the Lord.

_____

_____

_____

_____

_____

II. Comprehending the Lesson

A. Check the appropriate box to indicate your beliefs.

	Agree	Disagree
1. Credit cards should be paid off each month.	❏	❏
2. Couples should use "cents off" coupons at grocery stores.	❏	❏
3. Bankruptcy is a good way to get out of debt.	❏	❏
4. A family budget is a necessity.	❏	❏
5. Checkbooks should balance to the penny.	❏	❏
6. Vacations are more important than saving money.	❏	❏
7. It is okay to go into debt to buy a house.	❏	❏
8. A couple should plan the cost of their wedding and honeymoon together.	❏	❏
9. Gambling is a good recreational activity.	❏	❏
10. It is important to tithe.	❏	❏
11. It is okay to be unconcerned about money and not to think about financial matters.	❏	❏
12. Spouses should talk about money.	❏	❏

Financial Responsibility

	Agree / Disagree	
13. It is important to pay bills promptly.	❑	❑
14. One spouse should be able to have debts the other knows nothing about.	❑	❑
15. God's instructions should guide financial decisions.	❑	❑
16. Married couples should not ask their parents for money except in extreme circumstances.	❑	❑
17. Children should always have the latest fashions to wear.	❑	❑
18. It is okay to use credit cards in emergencies.	❑	❑
19. Couples should have joint checking accounts.	❑	❑
20. The husband should always control the budget.	❑	❑
21. Is not miserly to shop for discounts.	❑	❑
22. Tithes should be taken out first.	❑	❑
23. Wives should always earn less than their husbands.	❑	❑
24. It is a bad idea to go into debt at Christmas.	❑	❑
25. Parents should agree on allowances for children.	❑	❑

B. Your _____ and _____ should automatically be excluded from your usable income.

C. The percentages normally assigned to areas of monthly spending are:

_____ housing   _____ insurance

_____ food   _____ clothing

_____ transportation   _____ savings

_____ entertainment   _____ miscellaneous

III. Writing

A. Write one sentence describing each of the four financial principles.

1. God owns everything.

_____

_____

2. Plan ahead.

_____

_____

3. Keep accurate records.

_____

_____

4. Learn about financial matters.

_____

_____

B. Write one paragraph describing how credit cards
    can be dangerous to a marriage.

_____

_____

_____

_____

_____

_____

_____

_____

_____

13

Roots of Strife

Hatred stirs up strife, but love covers all sins.

Proverbs 10:12

Introduction

Couples often enter a marriage with a "happy-ever-after" glow. There is nothing wrong with that as long as they temper the illusion with realism. Married people, who are deeply in love and greatly respect each other, still have disagreements.

There are problems with relatives and friends. Couples undergo stress from illness or death. Careers change and jobs may be lost. Hectic schedules may separate spouses more than is good for the marriage. Priorities may change for one spouse and not for the other. One of the spouses may have had a dysfunctional family, which creates negative attitudes and behaviors. Hundreds of unexpected events and unanticipated stresses assault couples, daily tearing at the stability of their marriages.

Couples can overcome stress by approaching the problems honestly and without anger. They must follow Jesus' example of love and forgiveness.

Relatives

Almost every comedian tells mother-in-law jokes. One study indicated that the husband's mother causes as much trouble for a young couple as all the other in-laws combined. Much of this conflict is between the mother-in-law and the daughter-in-law and centers on competition for the attention of the son and husband. Most of the remaining conflict is about the proper way to rear children. The mother-in-law frequently questions the mother's child-rearing policies. Often she overindulges the grandchildren with gifts.

This stereotype of the poor relationship between a wife and mother-in-law can reveal some truth about the difficulty in establishing one family separated from two others. How does a newly married couple handle this? Sometimes not well. They must always remember the Biblical instruction, "Therefore shall a man leave his father and mother, and shall cleave to his wife . . . ." The newly formed family has to make decisions based on what is best for the sanctity of their family.

How much influence should family and friends have on decisions of the couple? This varies with each family. Below are some guidelines and principles which can help.

- Final decisions belong to the couple.
- Strive for a policy of harmony between the generations without allowing unwarranted interference in your marriage and family.
- Choose counsel from friends and family who can be objective when the couple needs and seeks advice.
- Seek Christian friends and family members who give advice in a humble spirit.
- Make family decisions based on love.

Serious stress often begins with the marriage plans and ceremony. Family and friends will offer advice from the choice of spouse to the color of the bridesmaids' dresses. The two future mothers-in-law may compete and conflict over decisions. It becomes more complicated when there is an ex-husband, or ex-wife and a new spouse. Who should sit where? Who should be invited? Whose granddaughter is the flower girl? Will it upset your cousin if he is not the best man? Which friends or relatives will be bridesmaids? The bride and groom always have to keep in mind, "Whose wedding it is" while trying to avoid as much conflict as possible.

Bible Truths

A peaceful, quiet atmosphere is characteristic of a godly home and when strife is continuous between family members, agreement to part company may be the only peaceful solution.

Genesis 45:4-9; 50:19-21

Willingness to forgive one another, and to see God's hand in the events of life can knit a family together. Joseph refused to blame his brothers for all that they had done to him many years before. Instead he gave God the glory for what He had done, and loaded his brothers with benefits.

Proverbs 11:29; 15:7, 25, 27; 18:19; 19:13; 21:9, 19

Here God through Solomon warns of a number of actions and attitudes which destroy the peaceful atmosphere of a godly home: a troubler, a greedy member, hatred, pride, an offended brother, contentiousness, a brawling woman.

Genesis 13:5-18; 14:11-16

God blessed Abram after he generously gave Lot first choice of the land and the two men separated, their shepherds and flocks. Later Abram showed his continued concern for his nephew by rescuing him from his captors. God blessed this attitude and action on Abram's part.

Genesis 21:10-12

God approved of the separation of Hagar and Ishmael from Abraham's household.

Genesis 31:1-3, 13, 17-22

God directed Jacob, with his family to leave Laban when they could no longer get along together.

Encyclopedia of Bible Truths for School Subjects
Dr. Ruth C. Haycock © ACSI

Society often depicts holidays, especially Thanksgiving and Christmas, as the happiest celebrations of the year. However, for many young families, these two holidays are the most stressful times they face. Each spouse's family competes for time with the couple and grandchildren. They become hurt when they think they have been slighted. Some couples eat four or more meals on Thanksgiving Day just to avoid hurting other people's feelings or breaking a tradition. They eat at her parents' home, at his parents' home, at their own home, and at grandparents' homes. Additional problems arise when there has been a divorce, remarriage, and potential bitterness among various family members. The old lyric, "Over the river and through the woods to grandmother's house we go!" almost needs a new verse stating which grandmother.

Christmas can add stress with relatives. Each household has some tradition or event that everyone must attend. Grandparents, who have opened presents on Christmas Eve for 35 years, expect their children and their mates to continue the tradition with them. The other father and mother-in-law expect their time. The newly-formed family has to do some creative scheduling to satisfy the wants of others and to establish its own traditions.

Couples must openly discuss how to celebrate holidays, or resentment will build. This can result in an argument or hurt feelings. The best solution is a compromise which respects the rights of the couple and the expectations of the relatives.

Schedules

Most people consider their lives to be "too busy." They do not have enough time for everything they "have to do." When this is true, personal conflicts arise. The people involved find themselves in stressful situations.

Schedule conflicts result from an individual's or family's responsibilities, commitments and interests. Responsibilities are those things which we must do, such as work, attend school, eat meals or sleep. Commitments are those things we choose to do, which obligate us to add them to our schedule, such as teach Sunday school, bake treats for school, coach basketball or sing in the church choir. Interests are those things we want to add to our schedule because they fill a physical, social, intellectual or emotional desire. We may read, watch television, have a party or go bowling. The last category is where most over-scheduling occurs for a family.

Everyone has the same amount of time each day. However everyone does not have the same number of responsibilities and commitments. Family members should prepare a schedule built around responsibilities and commitments. They should then identify common family interests.

A family schedule will usually work if members post it in a prominent place, if it is flexible in case of unforeseen events, and if it has weekly and monthly breakdowns. Problems occur when there is an imbalance of time for the three categories, when the family fails to coordinate the individual schedules of family members, and there is an unwillingness to follow the schedule by family members.

Society and Divorce

The ultimate stress to a family is the threat or actuality of a divorce. Once rare, there were 1.2 million divorces in the United States in 1994. Divorces have an impact on the couple involved, any children involved, and other relatives and friends. The threat of divorce in itself has become a root of strife in many families. Couples will use the ease of obtaining a divorce as a threat when problems arise or an argument escalates.

American attitudes toward divorce have changed dramatically since the mid-1900's. Secular society seems to celebrate the failure of marriage as a success. Disintegration and disaster has become synonymous with growth and triumph.

Bible Truths

Marriage is meant by God to be permanent — until the death of one partner.

Matthew 19:5; Mark 10:6-7

Jesus answering the Pharisees as they questioned Him about divorce: *6 But from the beginning of the creation God made them male and female. 7 For this reason a man shall leave his father and mother and be joined to his wife.*

Matthew 5:32; Luke 16:18

Under the Law, and in the Kingdom, to divorce a wife not guilty of fornication was to make her an adulteress. Also, to marry a divorced woman was to commit adultery. In other words, divorce was not approved under the Law.

Matthew 19:5-6; Mark 10:8-9

Jesus speaking to the Pharisees: *5 . . . The two shall become one flesh. 6 So then, they are no longer two but one flesh. Therefore what God has joined together, let not man separate.*

Romans 7:2-3

Here the law concerning the permanence of marriage is used to illustrate the relationship between law and grace. *2 For the woman who has a husband is bound by the law to her husband as long as he lives. But if the husband dies, she is released from the law of her husband.*

1 Corinthians 7:10-16

Written to Gentile Christians, three things are said about the permanence of marriage as God intends it: (1) a wife should not depart from her husband, and a husband should not put away his wife; (2) if a wife departs, she should not marry another man; (3) if a believer has an unbelieving spouse who is willing to continue, the believer should not separate.

Encyclopedia of Bible Truths for School Subjects
Dr. Ruth C. Haycock © ACSI

In the June 1982 issue of *New Woman,* authors John and Nancy Adam devalue marriage saying, "Yes, your marriage can wear out. People change their values and lifestyles. People want to experience new things. Change is part of life. Change and personal growth are traits for you to be proud of, indicative of a vital searching mind. You must accept the reality that in today's multi-faceted world it is especially easy for two persons to grow apart. Letting go of your marriage — if it is no longer good for you — can be the most successful thing you have ever done. Getting a divorce can be a positive, problem-solving, growth-oriented step. It can be a personal triumph."

Christians, especially those experiencing difficult times in their marriages, must be careful not to fall into the trap of thinking like the world. Society has made it easy to obtain a divorce. This does not mean that couples should choose divorce instead of solving their problems in marriage. Despite the clear principles set forth in the Bible and the best intentions of the Christian couples who marry each year, the divorce rate of believers continues to increase.

While most Christians recognize limited, justifiable reasons for divorce, the ideal is one man, one woman for one lifetime. They, therefore, resist looking for an answer in divorce. At the same time, they are sympathetic and empathize with those who have experienced divorce, choosing to encourage them toward growth in the Lord. There are many socio-logical and psychological reasons for the increase in the divorce rate among Christians. The major reason is the loss of commitment to a Christian understand-ing of the sanctity and permanence of marriage.

When problems occur in a marriage, Christians have three choices. They can divorce, choosing what appears to be the easiest way to stop problems. They can ignore the problems and contin-ue to be unhappy, while destroying their testimony to friends and families. They can be mature and responsible by admitting the problems and then work to reestablish an intimate and loving marriage.

Christians should not focus on whether there are legitimate reasons for divorce. Their focus should be on living in the will of God through a permanent marriage. This will help to ensure personal happi-ness, strong Christian homes and a stable society.

Dysfunctional Families

Some families have problems that cause them to be dysfunctional. Problems within individual members of a family can create serious strife that can destroy families. Christian family counselors and therapists characterize a dysfunctional family as one that has one or more of the following:

- One or both partners being unbalanced, preoccu-pied, emotionally restricted, frustrated or unrealistic in their views of the world.

- Partners and/or children who are addicted to alcohol or drugs.
- Partners who are workaholics.
- Partners who are consumed by rage or compulsion concerning things about which healthy people are casual.
- Immature partners who rely excessively on others for nurturing, ego-bolstering, advice and help.
- Partners who divorce, separate, fight viciously and feel bitter toward each other and marriage in general.
- Partners who remain together in a hostile relationship "for the sake of the kids" without trying to correct the relationship itself.
- Partners in an uncomfortable relationship with God. Or they may be intensely religious, believing that God will accept them if they look and think exactly right. They are extremely rigid in theology, thinking that the only correct way in which to relate to God is their way. These people are adamant that their children precisely follow the pattern they have established.

While those living in a dysfunctional family experience physical and emotional pains, the real tragedy is that the problems affect succeeding generations. The type of dysfunction may change from generation to generation. An alcoholic father may have a son who is a workaholic and a daughter who spends her way to bankruptcy. The alcoholic father has produced children who are dysfunctional in different ways. Like a weak thread in a piece of cloth, the dysfunction syndrome passes from one generation to the next, weaving a pattern of instability and pain.

Dysfunctions pass from one generation to the next for two basic reasons. Our ideal of family and adulthood is shaped by our childhood experience. Unless we make conscious effort to change, we are destined to repeat the family experience. We allow our childhood experience to determine our perceptions and choices. Christians who are members of dysfunctional families should undergo counseling in order to break the cycle.

Summary

Christian marriages can be threatened by a number of assaults including:

- poor communication,
- financial mismanagement,
- relationships with relatives,
- overburdened schedules,
- availability of divorce, and
- dysfunctional partners.

Overcoming these assaults can present huge challenges. Sometimes they seem so enormous that the potential for a successful marriage appears to be out of reach. However, a Christian couple can take confidence in cooperating with God Who has obligated Himself to accomplish His will in and through them. God provides this confidence in these verses:

- Jeremiah 29:11 — For I know the thoughts that I think toward you, says the LORD, thoughts of peace and not of evil, to give you a future and a hope.

- Philippians 1:6 — Being confident of this very thing, that He Who has begun a good work in you will complete it until the day of Jesus Christ.

- Philippians 2:13 — For it is God Who works in you both to will and to do for His good pleasure.

- Philippians 4:13 — I can do all things through Christ Who strengthens me.

One Plus One

Challenge Your Thinking

I. **Bible Link**

A. Compare and contrast the paragraph from the 1982 issue of *New Woman* with what Jesus said in Matthew 19:3-12.

_____

_____

_____

_____

_____

_____

_____

_____

B. Read Deuteronomy 24:1-4, Matthew 3-12, and 1 Corinthians 7:10-16. Write a one to two page summary of what the Bible teaches about marriage and divorce. Use a separate sheet of paper for your summary.

II. Comprehending the Lesson

A. Write the five principles that help to relieve strife for married couples.

1. _____

_____

2. _____

_____

3. _____

_____

4. _____

_____

5. _____

_____

B. Write five characteristics of a dysfunctional family.

1. _____

_____

2. _____

_____

3. _____

_____

4. _____

_____

5. _____

_____

C. Why is divorce not an immediate option for a Christian couple?

_____

_____

_____

_____

_____

D. What resources are available to a Christian
    couple to withstand assaults to their marriage?

    _____

    _____

    _____

    _____

    _____

III. Writing

A. Write a paragraph about the strife that can be
    caused when a married couple tries to please
    relatives.

    _____

    _____

    _____

    _____

    _____

    _____

B. Explain how a schedule can help to relieve strife in a family.

_____

_____

_____

_____

C. Write a paragraph explaining your own feelings about divorce

_____

_____

_____

_____

_____

_____

14

Joys and Challenges of Children

And you, fathers, do not provoke your children to wrath, but bring them up in the training and admonition of the Lord.

Ephesians 6:4

Introduction

It has never been easy to be a parent. Babies come into this world without written instructions. Parents have to learn on-the-job. Children are complex, with no guaranteed formulas that ensure successful outcomes. Parents, with two or more children, readily acknowledge that the child-rearing technique that was so successful with one of their offspring completely failed with another.

Newly married couples should have discussed the prospect and desire of having children during the courting and engagement steps of their relationship. Christian couples need to seek the Lord's direction and answer several questions. Do we want to have

Bible Truths

Children are a gift from God and therefore to be appreciated.

Genesis 4:1, 25

Eve recognized that her sons came from the Lord. So did Leah when Reuben was born (29-32) and later as she and Rachel talked about their condition (30:2-24); Esau credited God with his children, as he came to meet Jacob (33:5); Joseph, presenting his sons to his father said, *They are my sons whom God has given me in this place* (48:9).

Ruth 4:13-17

Boaz and Ruth, Naomi, and the neighbor women recognized God's gift of Obed to the couple and to the grandmother.

Job 1:21; 42:10-16

Job, when stripped of everything, still recognized the fact

that it was God Who had given both his children and his material goods, and now had taken them away. At the end, he recognized the Lord's goodness as well.

Psalm 127:3-5

3 Behold, children are a heritage from the LORD, the fruit of the womb is His reward. 4 Like arrows in the hand of a warrior, so are the children of one's youth. 5 Happy is the man who has his quiver full of them; They shall not be ashamed, but shall speak with their enemies in the gate.

Encyclopedia of Bible Truths for School Subjects
  Dr. Ruth C. Haycock © ACSI

children? Why do we want to have children? How many children should we have? When do we want our first child? If we cannot have children, do we want to adopt?

Statistical trends in the 1990's show that couples are marrying and having children later in life than their parents and grandparents did. This may help couples to be more stable in their relationships and to prepare for parenthood more effectively. Children do change the family structure and the relationship between husbands and wives. A couple who is secure in their relationship will be better prepared to handle the multitude of challenges that will occur after the arrival of children.

Blessings

Jesus loved children and gave them a special place during His ministry on earth. In Matthew 19:14, He told his disciples "Permit little children, and forbid them not, to come unto me; for such is the kingdom of heaven." Then He blessed the children. Parents are blessed from the time a child is in the mother's womb. The blessing of children for parents, the family and grandparents continues throughout the years.

Parents feel a special joy when the baby in the womb kicks for the first time. Another special time is the moment of birth. Babies give parents inexplicable joy. The beauty is that the joys continue as children grow and develop. Photograph albums and video cassette tapes abound with recorded memories of a baby's dedication to the Lord, first birthday, first step, first tooth and hundreds of other events.

Parents have the responsibility of rearing their children properly, but this responsibility pales when compared to the enjoyment of seeing their children grow and develop. There is a special pride in helping children prepare for school, in helping lead them to know the Lord, in teaching them to play games and in attending their school graduations.

Perhaps the climax of this enjoyment comes when parents experience the bitter-sweet joy of seeing their children marry and begin their own families. Then comes the happiness of being grandparents and the pride of seeing the principles which they have instilled in their children passed to another generation of their family.

Biblical Concepts

God devotes extensive portions of the Bible to the subjects of children and child-rearing. Jesus focused some of his most profound teachings around children. Before having children, Christian couples should study God's Word and consider the responsibilities of parenthood.

Basic Biblical concepts that parents need to understand are:

- the true nature of children,
- how to care for their children,
- what it means to provide for their children,
- how to respect their children, and
- what it means to forgive their children.

Two Natures

The Bible teaches that our original parents were created in the image of God. Thus, each member of humanity becomes an image-bearer of the King of kings. This is especially evident in our sense of spirituality, that internal vacuum which can be fulfilled only by the Holy Spirit resident in our lives after we receive Christ as Savior.

Bearing the image of God gives humans unique abilities not found in other life on earth. These are the abilities:

- to think, discern, evaluate and make judgments, which in turn modifies our behavior.
- to create, bringing order out of chaos.
- to communicate using elaborate, generative language in many forms.
- to accumulate knowledge, and, through reading and writing, to communicate that knowledge across space and generations of time.

Bible Truths

God holds parents responsible for their children — to teach them, to provide for them, to control them, to correct them.

Deuteronomy 6:6-9, 20-23; 11:18-21

In Israel, God commanded that there should be daily, casual and constant teaching: *7 You shall teach them diligently to your children, and shall talk of them when you sit in your house, when you walk by the way, when you lie down, and when you rise up.*

Proverbs 4:1-4,10-11, 22:6

1 Hear, my children, the instruction of a father, and give attention to know understanding. 2 For I give you good doctrine: do not forsake my law. 22:6 Train up a child in the way he should go, and when he is old he will not depart from it.

Ephesians 6:4

And you, fathers do not provoke your children to wrath, but bring them up in the training and admonition of the Lord.

Proverbs 29:15, 17

15 The rod and reproof give wisdom, but a child left to himself brings shame to his mother. 17 Correct your son, and he will give you rest; yes, he will give delight to your soul.

2 Corinthians 12:14

Paul to the church at Corinth, says: *14 . . . the children ought not to lay up for the parents but the parents for the children.*

1 Timothy 3:4-5, 12; Titus 1:6

Only a father whose children are under his control is qualified to be a pastor or deacon.

1 Timothy 5:8

Through this passage is dealing with widows in particular, the truth doubtless applies to other family members. *8 But if anyone does not provide for his own, and especially for those of his household, he has denied the faith and is worse than an unbeliever.*

Encyclopedia of Bible Truths for School Subjects
Dr. Ruth C. Haycock © ACSI

- to establish bonds and relationships with others leading to the establishing of families and societies.
- to consider abstract concepts of love, peace, eternity, beauty, character, justice and even the nature of thinking itself.

When Adam and Eve sinned, the original image became marred. Subsequently, mankind bares a sin nature that automatically places "self" at the center of the universe. Thus, every person has two natures. First is the image of God — with all its potential for service to God and others. Second is sin — with all its potential for evil and destruction.

The Bible teaches that children are not good at birth. Psalm 51:5 says, "Behold, I was brought forth in iniquity, and in sin my mother conceived me." In Ephesians 2:3, Paul states that all of us "... were by nature children of wrath, just as the others." Many parents have difficulty understanding that children possess a sin nature at birth that must be controlled and ultimately changed by the saving grace of Jesus Christ. When parents understand the sin nature in all children, they will begin to shape the child through benevolent authority given to them by God.

In Proverbs 22:6, the Bible instructs parents to "Train up a child in the way he should go, and when he is old he will not depart from it." In Psalms 1:1-3, we are reminded that children need nourishment the same as a young, growing tree. Parents do not fulfill their child-rearing duties by providing only food, shelter, clothing and an education. Children need spiritual instruction, emotional support and regular interaction with their parents. Parents must care for their children just as God cares for His children.

God instructs parents to provide for their children. (This does not mean giving them everything they want.) Paul says in 1 Timothy 5:8, "But if any provide not for his own, and especially for those of his own house, he hath denied the faith, and is worse than an infidel." Parents may have to sacrifice things they desire in order to provide for their children.

When parents are rearing their children in a Biblical manner, they must be careful to respect the children as creations of God. Part of this is addressed in Colossians 3:21, where fathers are instructed ". . . do not provoke your children, lest they become discouraged." Children will learn respect to the extent that they have experienced respect.

An intact, stable family provides the foundations for trust and love. As children experience a secure, consistent environment with parents who conscientiously respond to their needs, their own senses of confidence grow. From these early experiences of trusting parents, they can make a transition to trusting God, the eternal Father, Who is unfailing in meeting our deepest needs. In the same manner, children who experience warm, loving relationships in the home develop a sense of acceptance and affirmation of their innate value. Consequently, they more easily comprehend the love of God, His purposes and their potential contributions and places in the world.

The family also offers the opportunity for a child to learn forgiveness. In Luke 15:11, Jesus tells the parable of the prodigal son to illustrate the way in which parents should forgive children when they have made mistakes or hurt them. The father in this parable not only forgives his wayward son, but he restores his son to his proper place in the family. When a child errs, it is important that the appropriate punishment be rendered. However, it is much more important for the child to realize that the wrong behavior does not result in his being distanced from the family. His sin results in broken fellowship, but can never stop his being a son. As Jesus forgives His children, so should parents forgive their children.

Parenting Priorities

Before couples marry, they must commit together to the discipline necessary to establish a family. They must commit to maintaining a harmonious and loving relationship. This may seem simple to a newly married couple. Yet, it is not easy to achieve. Partners develop harmony in the home by daily committing their love to each other and by determining to fulfill their Biblical roles within the family.

One Plus One

Colossians 3:18-21 reminds parents of the important roles they play in the lives of their children. Children respond to the love their parents have for each other, as well as to the love the parents show to them. Children need to be loved, nurtured and disciplined by parents who realize that their children are God's children. These parents equate parenthood with Biblical stewardship. They know that children are not meant to hold the marriage together, provide for them in their old age or be companions when one spouse is away.

Parents readily acknowledge that each child is different. They must learn to respond to the individual differences in each child, just as Jesus responded to his Twelve Disciples according to their individual needs. He understood their frailties and errors, and always forgave them. Jesus did not allow Peter to drown when Peter doubted his own ability to walk on water. Jesus rebuked him, after having reached out His hand to save Peter. Parents have to build trust in their children. At the same time, they must rescue them from difficult situations and admonish them for failure to do the correct thing.

Parents soon learn that their children fail to keep promises. Rather than punish them for unkept promises, it is better to teach them not to make promises they cannot keep. Jesus knew that it was a rash, unkeepable promise when Peter said that he would go to prison and to death for Jesus (Luke

22:33). Jesus knew that Peter was impetuous. He dealt with this by simply telling Peter how he would deny knowing Him three times before morning. Peter protested, but learned his lesson later, when he heard the rooster crow and realized that he had denied knowing Jesus. In a different issue with Thomas, Jesus used another type of response. Thomas did not deny Jesus, but wanted proof that the Lord had risen. Jesus, in the most fatherly manner, had Thomas touch His wounds. Parents sometimes have to allow a child to prove for himself or herself those things which may be obvious to others.

An important priority for parents is giving their children wise advice and godly directions. Children do not know which road to follow, unless it is explained to them. They also must be given the knowledge and ability to follow those directions. In Matthew 10:1, Jesus gave His disciples ". . . power over unclean spirits, to cast them out, and to heal all kinds of sickness and all kinds of disease." Then in verses 8-11, He told them what he expected them to do and gave instructions to enable them to accomplish his directions. "Heal the sick, cleanse the lepers, raise the dead, cast out demons. Freely you have received, freely give. Provide neither gold nor silver nor copper in your money belts, nor bag for your journey, nor two tunics, nor sandals, nor staffs; for a worker is worthy of his food. Now whatever city or town you enter, inquire who in it is worthy, and stay there till you go out."

Parents must follow this example. What appears to be a simple directive such as, "Clean your room," can be a problem. The parents must have demonstrated how to clean, what tools to use and clearly defined what is meant by a clean room. By having the child recite his or her understanding of the instructions, some parents have a higher degree of success. The parent can then correct misunderstandings before there is a confrontation.

Summary

It is in the home where children learn their concepts of the basics of life. The parents, as the child's first models and teachers, are responsible to instill manners, obedience, respect, humility, honesty and diligence in their children. Children learn by observing their parents. Every parent is a model, whether it is good or bad. Parents who are Christians have the advantage of knowing Biblical principles and applying them to their own lives, thus passing these Christian principles on to their children through both direct and indirect instruction.

Challenge Your Thinking

I. **Bible Link**

A. Locate, list and describe five Biblical examples of Jesus illustrating parenting priorities in His work with the Twelve Disciples.

Verse _____

_____

_____

Verse _____

_____

_____

Verse _____

_____

_____

Verse _____

_____

_____

Verse _____

_____

_____

B. Read Ephesians 6:2-3. Then write a paragraph
    on the promise God makes to obedient children.

_____

_____

_____

_____

_____

_____

_ _

_____

_____

_____

_____

C. Read Hebrews 12:7-11. List five principles
   related to the discipline of children.

   1. _____

   2. _____

   3. _____

   4. _____

   5. _____

II. Comprehending the Lesson

A. List five blessings parents derive from their
   children.

   1. _____

   2. _____

   3. _____

   4. _____

   5. _____

B. List five Biblical concepts about children.

   1. _____

   2. _____

3. _____

4. _____

5. _____

C. List five responsibilities parents have in training their children.

1. _____

2. _____

3. _____

4. _____

5. _____

III. Writing

A. Write a paragraph describing ways in which you have been a blessing to your parents.

_____

_____

_____

_____

_____

_____

_____

_____

_____

B. Write a paragraph describing how you have
been a challenge to your parents.

_____

_____

_____

_____

_____

_____

_____

_____

C. Based on your paragraphs in A and B, make a list
of things you may or may not do with your own
children.

1. Will do

_____

_____

_____

_____

_____

2. Will not do

_____

_____

_____

_____

_____

15

Marriages That Endure

Therefore what God has joined together, let not man separate.

Mark 10:9

Introduction

A statistic about the rate of failure of marriages in the United States has been quoted and used many times — 50 percent of the marriages in this country will end in divorce. That can be interpreted to mean that if you marry this year, you have only a one in two possibility of an enduring, Biblical marriage. Well, there is good news. The statistic quoted gives only partial information about the rate of divorce.

It is true that in the year 1994, there were 2.5 million marriages and 1.2 million divorces. That appears to be almost a 50 percent failure rate. However, it is an overstatement of a statistic.

One Plus One

In January, 1994, there were already 54 million married couples in the United States, making a 1994 total of 56.5 million. With 1.2 million divorces, the divorce rate was only 2.2 percent. This is considerably lower than the over-stated statistic.

People want to be married. Ninety percent of those who divorce will remarry. Marriage is one of the most enduring institutions on earth. How do couples have lasting marriages? In a 1990 random survey of 3,000 women and 1,000 men, the Roper Institute asked, "What makes a good marriage?" Out of all the answers, one response was most common. Eighty-seven percent of the women and 84 percent of the men answered, "being in love."

It is clear that "being in love" is more than sexual passion. It is the deep, interwoven affection of two people who love, honor and cherish each other. It is the highest step in the journey couples make from Awareness through Marriage and the Family.

The deepening bond and commitment to each other can be expressed as couples follow this marriage creed.

I–nspire warmth

L–ighten the way
O–pen your heart
V–alue your union
E–xpress your trust

Y–ield to good sense
O–verlook mistakes
U–nderstand differences

Passionate Love

The first intense part of a relationship is the passionate stage of marriage. Two people in love want to be together all of the time. When they are together, they are ecstatic. Apart, they feel miserable. Poets and lyricists have written countless poems and songs about being in love; others will write millions more.

One good description of that first, passionate love appeared in the comic strip *Calvin and Hobbes*. Calvin, a young boy who converses with his stuffed tiger, Hobbes, asks, "What's it like to fall in love?"

Swinging his hands to demonstrate, Hobbes says, "First, your heart falls into your stomach and splashes your innards. All the moisture makes you sweat profusely. This condensation shorts the circuits to your brain, and you get all woozy. When your brain burns out all together, your mouth disengages and you babble like a cretin until she leaves."

Calvin responds with a sense of disappointment, "That happened to me once, but I figured it was cooties!"

It is doubtful that medical science will ever be able to fully explain why two people are attracted to each other. However, most people know when it happens to them. Some researchers believe that the initial attraction is a kind of match between a real person and a dreamed about person. Most people have endowed a fantasy mate with certain characteristics — physical appearance, intelligence, social skills and spiritual attributes. Then one day, someone appears who closely resembles the dream or fantasy person. When these people then marry, the passionate phase of a relationship can begin.

This passion is important to the relationship. Passionate love causes two people to focus almost totally on each other. The intense passion lasts long enough for them to begin building an enduring relationship. They learn about each other in this intimate period.

This passionate period is the honeymoon period of a marriage. It can last one month, one year, or longer. Elements of it will last a lifetime, although in part, it will subside. Couples with an enduring marriage are able to change from the excitement of the passionate period to a comfortable, deeply satisfying relationship. Sexual passion is transitory. It is only when a couple enjoys the other 99 percent of their time together that they can assure themselves of an enduring marriage.

This does not mean that passion and sex leave a marriage. They become part of the overall affection couples have for each other. Romance, passion and sex give way to real companionship, friendship and unity.

Companionate Love

In *Paths to Marriage*, Bernard I. Murstein describes companionate love as, ". . . a strong bond including tender attachment, enjoyment of the other's company and friendship. It is not characterized by wild passion and constant excitement, although these feelings may be experienced from time to time. The main difference between passionate and companionate love is that the former thrives on deprivation, frustration, a high level [of excitement] and absence. The latter thrives on contact and requires time to develop and mature."

Companionate love involves communication, commitment, caring, affection and support for one another. There are times of shared experiences and

Bible Truths

Husbands and wives are heirs together of God's grace — equal in importance and potential.

Matthew 28:5-10

It was women who were commissioned to go tell the disciples and Peter that He had risen. Note that they were commissioned by both the angel and by the Lord Himself.

Acts 1:13-14

The women were with the men in the upper room in prayer and later in preaching.

Acts 2:16-18

In Peter's sermon at Pentecost he referred back to Joel 2:28-32 in which the prophecy was made that God would pour out His Spirit on both men and women. In v. 16, he identifies the Day of Pentecost with part of the fulfillment of Joel 2.

Acts 8:3-4

When Saul persecuted the church, men and women went everywhere preaching the Word.

Romans 16:1-15; Hebrews 11:4-40

Note the mixture of names of both sexes; note also the specific commendations.

Galatians 3:26-28

26 For you are all sons of God through faith in Christ Jesus. 27 For as many of you were baptized into Christ have put on Christ. 28 There is neither Jew nor Greek . . . neither male nor female: for you are all one in Christ Jesus.

1 Peter 3:1-2

Wives have the privilege of winning their husbands to the Lord by their godly conduct.

1 Peter 3:7

Likewise you husbands, dwell with them with understanding . . . as being heirs together of the grace of life . . . .

Encyclopedia of Bible Truths for School Subjects
Dr. Ruth C. Haycock © ACSI

times of unhurried interaction that do not need to be charged with physical excitement.

These are characteristic of this type of love:

- Unselfish commitment to your partner's happiness;
- Compelling desire to enjoy what your partner enjoys;
- Maintenance of the three components of a relationship — one for them, one for her, and one for him;
- Freedom to share your real self with your partner; and
- Shared dreams and the plans for achieving them.

Christian Love

The Christian commitment of a couple is the only thing that can carry a marriage through the good times, bad times, births, deaths and other phases of life. With the Bible as their guide, a couple can overcome those things which cause marriage failure. Christian couples and families have another advantage, in that they enjoy Christian fellowship with others. They can rely upon fellow Christians to advise, pray for, support and counsel them through difficult situations.

Christians do not allow the world's standards and desires to erode the relationship they have built

235

together through Jesus Christ. Through prayer and studying the Word of God, they can overcome the daily temptations that assault marriages. When crises come, Christian couples have a sound foundation for surviving the most devastating situations.

Summary

In answer to the Pharisees, Jesus provides the summary on enduring marriage.

But from the beginning of the Creation, God made them male and female. For this reason a man shall leave his father and mother, and be joined to his wife, and the two shall become one flesh; so then they are no more two, but one flesh. Therefore what God has joined together, let not man separate.

Mark 10:6-9

Challenge Your Thinking

I. **Bible Link**

A. Faithfulness is a key ingredient in an enduring marriage. What do the following verses teach us about this subject?

1. Hebrews 13:4 _____

_____

2. 1 Corinthians 7:10-11 _____

_____

3. Proverbs 5:18 _____

_____

4. 1 Timothy 3:2 _____

_____

5. Exodus 20:14 _____

_____

One Plus One

B. Whether married or not, Solomon gives us food for thought, as a youth looks forward to a "life well lived." Read Ecclesiastes 12. Use your own words to complete this outline.

I. Admonition:

_____ v. 1

II. Rationale:
    A. The truth is _____

    _____ v. 2

    B. The illustration:

        1. poor eyesight _____ v. 2

        2. shaky, weak hands_____ v. 3

        3. osteoporosis _____ v. 3

        4. tooth loss_____ v. 3

        5. hearing loss _____ v. 3-4

        6. sleeping problems_____ v. 4

        7. unsteady gait _____ v. 5

        8. gray hair _____ v.5

        9. diminished sex _____ v. 5

        10. death _____ v. 5-7

III. Conclusion:

    A. On Earth — verse 13

_____

_____

    B. In Heaven — verse 14

_____

_____

IV. The Lesson for Me:

_____

_____

_____

_____

_____

_____

_____

_____

II. Comprehending the Lesson

A. Check the box you believe fits the appropriate category of a marriage relationship.

Activity	Passionate	Companionate	Both
Honeymoon	❑	❑	❑
Telling your spouse your deepest fears	❑	❑	❑
Planning for retirement together	❑	❑	❑
Hand-holding	❑	❑	❑
Long, involved kissing	❑	❑	❑
Shopping together	❑	❑	❑
Visiting your in-laws	❑	❑	❑
Private vacation with your spouse	❑	❑	❑
Nervousness on dates	❑	❑	❑
Spending an evening reading the Bible together	❑	❑	❑

B. List five characteristics of a companionate relationship.

1. _____

2. _____

3. _____

4. _____

5. _____

C. On what bases can a Christian couple expect to have an enduring marriage?

_____

_____

_____

_____

_____

_____

_____

_____

III. Writing

A. Why is the statement, "One in two marriages in America fails" not totally accurate?

_____

_____

_____

_____

_____

B. Why is a high divorce rate damaging to society as a whole?

_____

_____

_____

_____

C. Compare and contrast passionate and
    companionate love.

_____

_____

_____

_____

_____

_____

_____

_____

_____

_____

_____

Bibliography

Books:

Barna Research Group. *ACSI High School Student Survey Report and Analysis*. Whittier, California: ACSI, 1990.

Burkett, Larry. *How to Manage Your Money*. Chicago: Moody, 1975.

Coleman, William. *Before the Ring*. Grand Rapids, Michigan: Discovery House, 1995.

Dobson, James. *Love for a Lifetime*. Sisters, Oregon: Multnomah Books from Questar Publishers, Inc., 1993.

Dobson, James. *What Wives Wish Their Husbands Knew about Women*. Wheaton, Illinois: Tyndale House Publishers, Inc., 1975.

Fryling, Alice and Robert. *A Handbook for Married Couples*. Downers Grove, Illinois: InterVarsity Press, 1994.

Gibbs, Dr. Ollie E. and Keenan, Dr. Derek J. *Shaping the Next Generation*. Association of Christian Schools International, 1992.

Hardin, Jerry D. and Sloan, Dianne C. *Getting Ready for Marriage*. Nashville: Thomas Nelson Publishers, 1995.

Haycock, Ruth C. *Encyclopedia of Bible Truths for School Subjects*. Whittier, California: ACSI, 1993.

Mace, David R. *Getting Ready for Marriage*. Nashville: Abingdon Press, 1994.

Muerstein, Bernard I. *Paths to Marriage*. San Mateo, California: Sage Publications, 1986.

Parrott, Les III and Leslie. *Saving your Marriage Before It Starts*. Grand Rapids, Michigan: Zondervan Publishing House, 1995.

Richmond, Gary and Bode, Lisa. *Ounce of Prevention*. Ann Arbor, Michigan: Servant Publications, 1995.

Roberts, Wes and Judy, and Wright, H. Norman. *After You Say "I Do"*. Eugene, Oregon: Harvest House Publishers, 1979.

Roberts, Wes and Wright, H. Norman. *Before You Say "I Do"*. Eugene, Oregon: Harvest House Publishers, 1978.

Wheat, Ed and Perkins, Gloria Oakes. *Secret Choices*. New York: Harper Paperbacks, 1989.

Magazines:

"Risky Business." Freeman, Patricia. *People Magazine*, New York: November 1990.

Newspapers:

"Dear Abby." Van Buren, Abigail. *Chicago Tribune*, Chicago, 1995

Research Poll:

"Teenage Sexuality." *Time*/*CNN*. Atlanta and New York, 1994.

Bible Version:

All verses and excerpts in the text are taken from the New King James Version, Thomas Nelson Publishers, unless otherwise noted.

Additional Resources:

This is a very small list of some of the excellent books available on the topics of Dating, Family, Children and Sexuality. Each year new books are published adding to the tremendous collection of Christian literature on these topics. It is very beneficial to keep up with what is new and yet not lose sight that the Bible must be the final authority.

Barna, George. *Future of the American Family*. Moody Press, 1993.

Dobson, Dr. James and Bauer, Gary L. *Children at Risk*. Word Publishing, 1990.

Christenson, Larry. *The Christian Family*. Bethany Fellowship, 1970.

Gilder, George. *Men and Marriage*. Pelican Publishing Company, 1989.

Ford, Edward E. *Why Marriage?* Argus Communications, 1974.

Hendricks, Howard. *Heaven Help the Home*. Victor Books, 1975.

Huggett, Joyce. *Dating, Sex and Friendship*. InterVarsity Press, 1985.

Malcolm, Kari Torjesen. *Building Your Family to Last*. InterVarsity Press, 1987.

Piper, John and Gruden, Wayne, eds. *Recovering Biblical Manhood and Womanhood*. Crossway Books, 1991.

Schaeffer, Edith. *What Is a Family?* Fleming H. Revell Company, 1975.

Talley, Jim, and Reed, Bobbie. *Too Close Too Soon*. Thomas Nelson Publishers, 1990.

Warren, Ph.D, Neil Clark, *Finding the Love of Your Life*. Focus on the Family, 1992.

Wright, Norman. *Family Is Still a Great Idea*. Vine Books, Servant Publications, 1992.

Wright, Norman. *Inlaws, Outlaws*. Harvest House Publishers, 1977.

Wright, Norman and Inman, Marvin. *A Guidebook to Dating, Waiting and Choosing a Mate*. Harvest House, 1978.

Yorkey, Mike, ed. *Growing a Healthy Family*. Wolgemuth and Hyatt Publishers, 1990.

NOTES

NOTES

NOTES

NOTES

NOTES

NOTES

NOTES

NOTES